Facts about Norway

16th EDITION 1977-1978

SCHIBSTED

CONTENTS

Facts about Norway — 16th
edition 1977.
1st—16th edition: 352 000 copies
printed.
Published by the newspaper
Aftenposten, Oslo, in co-operation
with the Royal Ministry of Foreign
Affairs.
Editors: Ola Veigaard og Elin Krog.
© by Chr. Schibsteds Forlag,
Oslo 1977.

Printed in Norway by
A.S John Grieg, Bergen.
ISBN 82-516-0659-4
The statistics contained in the
booklet are based on the latest
available official figures and data.
Where not otherwise specified
English weights and measurements
are used. All values are stated in
Norwegian kroner (kr).

Country and People

Position:

Northernmost point — 71° 11' 8'' N.Lat.
Southernmost point — 57° 57' 31'' N.Lat.
Westernmost point — 4° 30' 13'' E.Long.
Easternmost point — 31° 10' 4'' E.Long.
North Cape — 71° 10' 21'' N.Lat.

Land frontiers etc.	2 531 km
— Sweden	1 619 km
— Finland	716 km
— USSR	196 km
Shortest distance north/south	1 752 km
Mainland coast length ca.	21 112 km
— minus fjords etc.	2 650 km
Country's greatest width	430 km
Country's smallest width	6.3 km

Area:	
Norway	386 308.1 km²
— Spitzbergen	62 049.5 km²
— Jan Mayen	372.5 km²
Norway excluding Spitzbergen & Jan Mayen	323 886.1 km²
Bouvet Island	58.5 km²
Peter I's Island	249.2 km²
Queen Maud Land	
200 nautical mile economic fishing zone	900 000 km²

The Country

Norway (in Norwegian: **Norge** — originally **Nordvegr,** meaning «the northern way») constitutes the western part of the Scandinavian peninsula, of which it covers about 40 %. The country is the fifth largest in Europe, while population density is next-lowest in Europe, after Iceland. In the east the country borders on Sweden, Finland and the Soviet Union, and otherwise has the sea as its boundary, with an exceptionally long coast line. Along the coast there are numerous islands (about 50 000, of which only 2 000 are inhabited) and nearly three quarters of the area is unsuitable for habitation or cultivation.

Oslo, the capital lies about 60° N. This latitude runs north of Scotland, through central Canada and

southern Alaska. Norway's most northern town, Hammerfest, is also the most northerly in the world, lying on 70°39'89'' N. latitude. The Arctic Circle crosses near the middle of Norway. Northern Norway is well known to tourists as «The land of the Midnight Sun».

Topography

Norway is a part of the great Fenno-Scandinavian bedrock area of the Caledonian mountain range. Most of the bedrock is in Swedish territory while Norway has most of the Caledonian rock type. Peculiar to Norway are the continental Devonian deposits and the Permian sediments and volcanic rock types in the depression around the Oslo region.

Four fifths of Norway is more than 150 metres above sea level, the average height a.s.l. being 500 metres (compared with 300 metres in the rest of Europe). In spite of this, most of the topography is not alpine. Most of the country con-

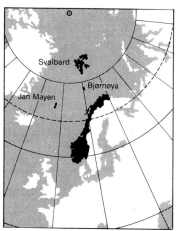

Norway and the Norwegian Arctic territory.

sists of treeless high plateaux, with numerous lakes, one of them Lake Hornindalsvatn, the deepest lake in Europe. The land area of which Norway is a part slopes gradually towards the east and drops steeply into the sea in the west.

The **Dovre** Mountains, the general direction of which is W—E, divide the country naturally in a northern and a southern part, while the latter is divided in a western and an eastern part by the **Langfjellene** Mountains (N—S). The mountain chain **Kjølen** runs N—S along the greater part of the Norwegian—Swedish border.

Glaciers and rivers of the Ice Age cut **valleys** in the mountains, long and sloping towards east and south, short and steep towards the west. They are continued by the **fjords,** which are usually narrow and penetrate far into the country — as far as 183 kilometres.

There are 1700 glaciers in Norway, covering a total area of 1 300 sq. miles.

The highest **waterfalls** are found in western Norway. The rivers of the interior do not run so swiftly, but many of these falls have a greater volume of water.

Flora and Fauna

Norway's flora is richer (about 2 000 species) than might be expected from the country's location. Most of the plants are also found in other countries, with only a few mountain plants being peculiar to Norway.

The predominating trees in Norwegian forests, which cover nearly one quarter of the country, are **spruce** and **pine,** but **birch** and other deciduous trees are found even in mountainous districts. Vegetation is richest in the southeastern districts, the deep forests of the main valleys forming the basis of Norwegian lumber industry. The conifers are seldom found above 800—1 000 m. Wild berries,

particularly **blueberries** and **cranberries,** grow in the woodlands. **Cloudberries,** which are little known outside Scandinavia, are gathered in the mountains.

Of animal life, the marine fauna is of considerable importance to the country, large districts being almost entirely dependent on fisheries. Of land animals the **bear** is almost extinct, while **elk** is found mainly in southeastern Norway and Trøndelag. **Reindeer** is the most important domestic animal in Finnmark. There are many species of animals of prey, such as **wolf, fox, lynx, otter.** Game birds are found both in the valleys and in the mountains, the **ptarmigan** (grouse) being the most common. Fresh water fish such as **trout** are found in practically all rivers and lakes throughout the country, while **salmon** is rarely caught elsewhere than in certain typical «salmon rivers».

Multitudes of sea birds nest on the coast of northern Norway. The nesting cliffs on the west and north coast, which are inhabited by thousands of birds, are among the country's tourist attractions.

Many of the birds of Norway are migratory, hatching in Norway, but living in more southern parts of the world for most of the year. Migration is also common with certain species of fish such as mackerel.

Bear, wolf and mountain fox are totally protected, while wolverine is protected only in southern Norway.

National Parks

Norwegians are in the happy position of having access to practically all lake and sea shores, and to vast forest lands and mountain areas. About 96 % of the country is open to the general public.

However, the increasing demands of a growing population for

sites for housing, roads and development of hydro-electric plants are having detrimental effects on forests, lakes, flora and wildlife.

The conservation of these assets is increasingly becoming a public issue, and several private societies as well as government agencies have been formed for this purpose. We have 13 national parks, and there are plans for adding to their number. **Rondane** and **Børgefjell** are among the most famous. A great many areas, of interest because of their flora and fauna, are or will be protected by law as nature reserves. Three national parks, two nature reserves and fifteen bird sanctuaries have been established in Svalbard.

Climate

There are many different types of climate in Norway. This is so on account of the country's geographical situation between 58° and 71° N, because of the varying topography, and because of strong prevailing westerly winds and the Gulf Stream along the west coast of Norway.

Along the entire length of the west coast from Lindesnes to Lofoten, the climate is exceptionally mild during the winter, with mean temperatures of 1—2° C. In Lofoten, mean temperature in January is low. In Finnmark, mean temperature in the winter is about ÷ 14° C, on the Røros high plateau it is about ÷ 10° C. Along the coast, mean temperature in the summer is not very high, about 13—14° C in southern Norway, and about 9° C in East Finnmark. The districts around Oslo and the Oslo Fjord have the highest mean temperature, 15—17° C. The highest temperature ever recorded in Norway is 35.6° C, the lowest ÷ 51° C.

Because of the prevailing westerly winds, the western part of Norway receives the greatest amount of precipitation. Some districts in that part of the country get about 3 000 mm annually, whereas a few inland districts get only 300—400 mm annually.

The Midnight Sun

The midnight sun is the term used to describe the phenomenon whereby the sun keeps above the horizon all day. That part of Nor-

Midnight sun, whole orb. Dark period

	Midnight sun	Dark period
Spitzbergen (Longyearbyen)	21/4—22/8	26/10—16/2
North Cape ..	14/5—29/7	18/11—24/1
Hammerfest ..	16/5—27/7	21/11—22/1
Tromsø	20/5—23/7	27/11—15/1
Bodø	7/6—8/7	15/12—29/12

Some Meteorological Dates

Temperatures in centigrade (Fahrenheit equivalents in brackets)						
	Mean temperatures		Extreme temperatures			Pre- cip.*
	Annual	January	July	Max.	Min.	
Oslo..	5.9 (43)	—4.7 (34)	17.3 (63)	35.0 (95)	—26.4 (—16)	42 in
Bergen	7.8 (46)	1.5 (35)	15.0 (59)	31.8 (89)	—15.1 (+ 5)	126 in
Trondheim ..	4.9 (41)	—3.4 (26)	14.4 (58)	35.0 (95)	—26.1 (—15)	49 in
Tromsø	2.9 (37)	—3.5 (26)	12.4 (54)	30.2 (86)	—18.4 (— 1)	59 in

* Max. precipitation in one year. Mean temperatures are during the normal period 1931—1960. The coldest areas are the Finnmark and Røros plateaux which on the average have 230—245 days a year with a temperature below freezing point. Highest recorded temperature in Norway is 35.6°C = 96°F, (Nesbyen), lowest ÷ 51.4°C = ÷ 61° F (Karasjok).

way which is north of the Polar Circle will experience a certain period of the summer with mid-night sun, and a corresponding period in the winter when the sun remains below the horizon with attendent darkness. At the beginning and end of the periods only a part of the sun will be visible in the southern part of the area north of the Polar Circle.

Population

Population: 4 017 231 (1976, estimated), which is equal to 12.4 inhabitants per sq. km (32.13 per sq. mile) — the dependencies not included. Or, to put it in another way — if the area were divided equally, there would be almost 100 000 sq. metres (eq. 25 acres) for each Norwegian.

Approx. 55% of the population live in rural districts, 45% in towns and built-up areas.

Man has lived in Norway for at least 10 000 years, but the country did not become really settled until historical times. The majority of the population today belong to the Nordic race — tall, fair, long-skulled people, and most of them have blue eyes. On the west and south coasts the population is of intermixed Alpine and Nordic stock, while here and in the southeastern forest districts, and in the far north there are also a number of people of Baltic origin, whose ancestors immigrated from Finland. In northern Norway the latter group **(kvener),** about 7 000 in number, has maintained its distinctive characteristics. In the north there is also a minority group of about 20 000 Lapps **(samer),** whose culture and language differ greatly from Norwegian culture and language. Dark hair, dark eyes and short stature are some of the anthropological characteristics often found in the population of the far north, and are an inheritance from the Lapps, who have been living there since pre-historic days.

Norway also has a number of foreign workers who have gradually been granted permanent residence permits — and many have become Norwegian citizens.

Norway has, together with the other Scandinavian countries and the Netherlands, the highest expectation of life in the world.

Main Cities

Oslo, the capital of Norway, has a poplation of 462 497 and covers a total area of 175 sq. miles. Founded about 1048. Seat of the King, Government and Parliament

Vital Statistics

	1900	1925	1950	1975	1976
Live births per 1000 population	26.7	19.7	19.1	14,1	13.3
Marriages per 1000 population	6.8	5,9	8.3	6.5	6.3
Average age at first marriage. Men	27.7	28.1	29.3	25.3	25.5
Women ..	25.7	25.6	26.4	22.9	22.9
Divorces per 100 marriages	0.7	4.2	8.5	21.5	22.9
Deaths per 1000 population	15.8	11.1	9.1	10.5	10.0
Deaths during first year per 1000 live births	90.5	50,2	28.2	11,1	10.4
Excess of births over deaths per 1000 population	10.9	8,6	10.0	4,1	3.3
Expectation of life Men	50.4	60.98	69.3	71,1	–
Women	54.14	63.8	72.7	78.0	–
Growth of Population					
Total in 1000	2 240	2 755	3 279	4 017	4 035
In towns, %	28.0	–	32.2	44.5	44.4

and the Supreme Court. The country's leading industrial city and most important commercial and shipping town.

Bergen (pop. 212 755). Norway's second largest city, is an old shipping and trading city and the cultural centre of Western Norway. **International Summer Festival** in May/June.

Trondheim (pop. 135 558). Important centre of trade, industry and shipping. The cathedral **Nidarosdomen** is the national shrine of Norway.

Stavanger (pop. 87 360) is presently the centre for on-shore activities concerning oil exploitation in the Norwegian sector of the North Sea. Seat of Statoil. Various industries, shipbuilding, fish processing etc.

Kristiansand (pop. 60 037). The «capital» of the south coast and centre of industry, trade and shipping.

Drammen (pop. 50 821). Administration centre for Buskerud county. Next to Oslo and Sarpsborg, Norway's biggest export point for timber products.

Skien (pop. 47 345). Trade centre of Telemark county. Birthplace of Henrik Ibsen, the famous Norwegian playwright and poet.

Tromsø (pop. 44 409). Covers bigger area than any other Norwegian town. A port of departure for several great Arctic expeditions. Seat of northernmost university in the world, now being established.

Ålesund (pop. 40 941). Norway's largest fishing port with a large fishing fleet and a number of processing plants.

Notes on History

800—900. Activities of the Vikings increase. The small Norwegian agrarian communities are organized into larger administrative and military regions.

875 (approx.). Small Viking settlements established in the Hebrides, the Isle of Man, the Shetlands and the Orkneys, England, Ireland and Normandy.

900 (approx.). Unification of the Realm. Battle of Hafrsfjord. King Harald Hårfagre (Fairhair) first supreme ruler of all Norway.

1000 (approx.). Greenland and America discovered, the latter by Leiv Eiriksson. Christianity introduced to Norway. Norway intermittently under Danish rule.

1030. King Olav Haraldsson killed in battle when trying to re-establish himself as king of Norway. Later on becomes Norway's patron saint. Consolidation of the monarchy under his son, Magnus (the Good), who 1042—47 is also king of Denmark.

1066. King Harald Hårdråde killed in battle of Stamford Bridge in the attempt to become king of England. This was the last Viking raid.

1130—1240. The dual system of succession, combining heredity and election. leads to civil war.

1152. Norway becomes separate bishopric, with archbishop's see at Nidaros (Trondheim).

1163. First coronation of a Norwegian king (Magnus V). Under new law of succession the Church is to decide between pretenders to the throne.

1194. King Sverre Sigurdsson comes into conflict with the Church and is excommunicated by the Pope.

1217—1263. End of civil wars, followed by a period of greatness for Norway (Iceland and Greenland dependencies of the Crown), also culturally — Snorre Sturlasson writes the Norwegian sagas.

1274—1276. King Magnus «Lawmender» codifies the laws of Norway.

1319—1360. Personal union with Sweden.

1349—1350. «Black Death» wipes out half the population. Economy deteriorates. Hanseatic merchants dominate trade.

1380. Union with Denmark which lasts till 1814.

1397. Union of Kalmar. Sweden joins the Danish-Norwegian union. The triple union continues, with intervals, until 1521.

1468—1469. The Orkney and the Shetland Islands mortgaged to the King of Scotland.

1563—1570. Nordic Seven Years' War.

1709—1721. Nordic Great War.

1807—1814. War against England and Sweden. Blockade and famine.

1811. First Norwegian university founded, opened 1813.

1814. Sweden forces Denmark to cede Norway. Norwegians refuse to recognize treaty. National Assembly convenes and adopts Constitution (May 17th), Danish prince elected King of Norway. War with Sweden July—August. King resigns and the first Norwegian Storting agrees to union with Sweden (1814—1905).

1837. Municipal self-government introduced.

1866—1873. First great emigration period with more than 100,000 emigrants, mainly to USA.

1884. Parliamentary government introduced.

1887. Jury system introduced.

1898. Universal male suffrage.

1900—1910. Second great emigration period (200 000 emigrants). Total overseas emigration from Norway: 880 000.

1905. Union with Sweden dissolved and Norway becomes independent. Prince Carl of Denmark elected King and takes the name of Haakon VII.

1913. Women's Parliamentary suffrage.

1914—18. Norway neutral in World War I, but merchant navy suffers great losses.

1925. Svalbard (Spitzbergen) placed under Norwegian sovereignity.

1940. Germany invades Norway April 9th. Fighting in Southern Norway until May 5th and in Northern Norway until June 7th. The King, the Crown Prince and the Government leave the country with the authority of Storting to continue the fight from London.

1940—45. Small Norwegian fighting units transferred from Norway form the nuclei of the Free Norwegian Forces, which are reinforced by recruits escaped from occupied Norway, Norwegians abroad and the merchant navy. Regime of terror, with concentration camps, introduced by Nazis, reprisals following acts of sabotage, and executions of political prisoners and hostages. In 1944, Norwegian refugees in Sweden set up fighting force.

1945. Surrender of German forces May 8th. The Storting ratifies UN Charter November 16th.

1949. Norway joins NATO.

1952. The Nordic Council, consisting of parliamentarians from Denmark, Finland, Iceland, Norway and Sweden, is established.

1957. King Haakon VII dies and is succeeded by Olav V.

1959. Norway joins the European Free Trade Association (EFTA).

1962 and **1967.** Norway applies for membership of the European Communities (EC).

1970. Norway starts negotiations with EC.

1971. Commercial oil drilling started in the North Sea.

1972. In an advisory referendum on Common Market membership Norway says NO to joining EC.

1973. Trade agreement with EC ratified by Norway.

1977. Norway extends her fishing limits from 12 to 200 nautical miles.

Government

Norway is a parliamentary democracy with a monarchical form of government. The political centre of gravity is in the National Assembly, the Storting. Its majority has wide authority to step in with regard to the most varied aspects of community life.

But even if the people's elected representatives may be said to have the last word in this way, the Norwegian society has become so complicated that a wide range of duties have had to be passed over to those who are permanently employed by the official administration. The administration, is however, watched over at all times by the Press and by those parties which form the Opposition. In addition to this a special Ombudsman has been appointed to deal with complaints from citizens who feel that they have been unfairly dealt with by the bureaucracy.

A high degree of private interest organisation also characterises today's Norway. Both employees and employers have long ago formed large, nationwide organisations, and the same is also true of producers of agricultural and fishing wares. The wage and price levels are, to a very great extent, fixed through agreements between the organisations in respect of the whole country, and partly between these and the State. The Storting, or the Government with the Storting's authority, has the formal right to intervene in the agreements, but refrains from doing so in practice, where possible, since adverse public opinion may be to their detriment at the following election. Norway may

The National Assembly at Eidsvold concludes the work on Norway's new Constitution, 17 May, 1814. This is Norway's national day.

therefore be said to have an extremely complicated government system. The Government and its administration is dependent upon a legislative assembly split up into political parties. The agreements which are concluded by organisations and by individual citizens, in keeping with the dispositions of individuals and companies generally, affect political conditions to a great extent. There is, therefore, a close correlation and interchange between State administration and community life generally.

THE CONSTITUTION

In political terms, Norway's modern history tends to be dated from 1814, when the country's Constitution was adopted. It is one of the world's oldest constitutions, in that it still remains the basis for the country's political system, even though it has undergone considerable amendment. The amendments have taken place both by means of formal resolutions, and also as a result of constitutional custom.

The Constitution, in its original form, had features which were partly borrowed from the Constitution of the United States, partly from Great Britain and partly from France after the revolution of 1789. The constitutional practice in Norway today is most like the British, because the function of the Monarch is primarily a symbolic one, while the Government is answerable to the Storting.

The Constitution pre-supposes three government authorities: the King and Government (the executive power), the Storting (the legislative power) and the Courts (the judicial power). Among the duties of the Supreme Court is the protection of the Constitution, in that the Law, as in the case of the United States, can overrule resolutions passed by the Storting, when these are found by the Law to be at variance with the Constitution. The Norwegian Supreme Court has, however, limited itself in this respect to exercising its right to a minimal degree.

Proposals for amendments to the Constitution must be submitted before the Storting, and may not be dealt with until a new General Election has been held, whereupon the proposal must gain a two-thirds majority in order to be passed by the next Storting.

The Constitution contains no regulations regarding referenda, but specific questions have been decided during the course of this century on the basis of nationwide advisory referenda. These have covered such wide-ranging questions as whether the form of government should be monarchical or republican in 1905, the question of Prohibition during the years between the two world wars as well as the question of Norwegian membership of the European Communities in 1972. After a majority had shown itself to be against membership, the relationship between Norway and the EC was regularised via a trade agreement.

General franchise

General franchise obtains in respect of elections and referenda. As early as 1814 the original Constitution contained clauses governing the right to vote which were very comprehensive for the age, but which still failed by a long way to cover all citizens. This right was, however, extended several times and covered all adult males by the end of the century. In the case of local alchohol plebiscites, women too were given the right to vote, and at the beginning of the present century they were also granted it at local elections. Finally, in 1913, universal adult suffrage was introduced in respect of

General Elections. The voting age has been reduced on several occasions, first of all in 1920 from 25 to 23 years, and subsequently to its present level of 20 years. The question of whether it should be further reduced to 18 years is currently being discussed.

A General Election to the Storting is held every four years. Local elections are held between every parliamentary election, so that there are nationwide elections held in Norway every other year: Parliamentary election autumn 1977, local elections throughout the country in the autumn of 1979, new Parliamentary election 1981, etc. This regularity has obtained throughout several decades. At the parliamentary elections the poll is in excess of 80% of the electorate, while the turnout for local elections has been about ten per cent lower during recent years.

THE STORTING

The Storting sits for the whole four year period for which it is elected, since the Constitution contains no clause in respect of dissolution. Neither are there any byelections held, since deputies take over in the case of deaths or other causes whereby a seat becomes vacant.

The Storting consists of one chamber. When legislation or matters affecting the Constitution are being discussed, the Storting is split into two divisions, the Odelsting and the Lagting. An important factor in the work of the national assembly is the apportionment of the Storting representatives on the various committees. These are apportioned according to subject matter, in accordance with the Government's division into ministries, and the committees carry out a great proportion of the parliamentary legislative, budgetary and controlling activities.

The Storting consists of 155 members. The representatives are elected on a county basis. The Northern counties return 38 representatives, the Western and Southern counties 49 and the Eastern counties 68. From among the latter, 15 are returned from the capital, Oslo, which is the only purely city constituency. Seen in comparison with the distribution of population, the more remote, thinly-populated areas, are given greater representation than the areas which are adjacent to the country's geographical administrative centre.

The Members of the Storting feel, to a considerable extent, that they represent the various districts from which they are elected.

The preparatory work with the Storting's affairs is conducted in specialist committees and in meetings of the parliamentary party groups. These are not open to the public. The arguments in the Storting, the official debates and votes, besides the queries and parliamentary questions directed at the Government, contribute widely to the formulations of official opinion. These have always been covered extensively by the press.

THE KING

King Olav V, born in 1903, has reigned since 1957, when he succeeded his father Haakon VII who had sat on the throne since 1905. The King symbolises the unity of the country. He presides over the Cabinet, but has otherwise no political function, apart from intervening in the event of the apportionment of elected representatives from the various parties making it uncertain which of the parties should be called upon to form an administration which would be able to cooperate with the Storting.

King Olav is the Commander-in-

King Olav V.   *Crown Prince Harald.*

Chief of the country's armed forces. Today this is of mere symbolic significance, although the right was actually invoked during the second world war. The King can use his right of veto to suspend legislation. He is the Head of the Church of Norway, to which he himself and at least half of his Cabinet must belong. In Law, the King can do no wrong. He cannot be censored or indicted. The throne is hereditary, succession being in direct male descending line.

The Royal Family

King Olav was married to Märtha, Princess of Sweden, who died in 1954. The marriage resulted in three children, the Princesses Ragnhild and Astrid, who are married to Norwegian commoners, and Crown Prince Harald, born 1937 and married in 1968 to a

Norway's Royal Family live at Skaugum; west of Oslo. Here we see Crown Prince Harald (left) with Princess Märtha Louise on his knee, and (right) Crown Princess Sonja with Prince Haakon Magnus.

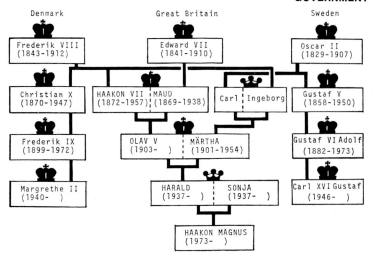

Interrelationship between the Norwegian and other European royal families.

Norwegian commoner, Miss Sonja Haraldsen. Crown Prince Harald and Crown Princess Sonja have two children, Princess Märtha Louise, born 1971, and Prince Haakon Magnus, born 1973. Their residence is at Skaugum, some kilometres West of Oslo, while King Olav remains at the Oslo Palace in the centre of the capital.

POLITICAL PARTIES

The Norwegian party system, which constitutes an important part of the country's political life, may be said to have the properties, in part, of both a multi-party and a two-party system. There are altogether 8 parties which are represented in the Storting, and there is a dividing line between the parties in respect of their programmes which is expressed in a socialistic and non-socialistic philosophy respectively.

The socialistic side is represented by two parties of some significance, — the Norwegian Labour Party and the Socialist Left Party, with 62 and 16 representatives respectively during the 1973—1977 period. On the non-socialist side the three largest parties are the moderate-Conservative Right, the agrarian Centre Party and the Christian Democrats. The two sides have had about the same amount of support from among the electorate during the last 15 years, and there have been certain changes in the relative strengths. However, quite large changes have taken place in the two camps during the 1970's, and this has again been expressed in large parliamentary shifts.

In order to gain an insight into the relationship, the Norwegian electoral system has to be taken into consideration. It is built on the principle of proportional representation. Each party should have a share of the seats in the national assembly which are in relation to its share of the votes, but in such a way that the system is applied with certain reservations. The large and the medium-

13

GOVERNMENT

sized parties receive greater representation in the Storting than that which corresponds mathematically with their share of the votes. This situation is justified by the desire to avoid the complications which arise if a country's national assembly becomes split up into myriad small parties.

The diagram below shows the partywise composition of the Storting during the four year period from the Autumn 1977 until Autumn 1981. The seats which are listed under 'Others' are divided between three non-socialist parties. The Norwegian Communist Party joined forces with the Socialist Left Party for a time, but subsequently broke out again as an independent party. Around 1960, when they were last represented at the Storting, they had about 60 000 votes.

No individual party has had an absolute majority in the national assembly since 1961. From 1965 until 1971 the country had a government composed of four non-socialist parties who together commanded a majority. The country has subsequently had minority governments, including, from 1973 a Government of the Norwegian Labour Party which has received

Distribution of votes, election 1977	Votes Autumn 1977		Stortings representatives	
	Total	Per cent	Total	Per cent
The Norwegian Labour Party	962 728	42.4	76	43.3
Social Left Party	94 016	4.1	2	1.3
Conservative Party	560 025	24.7	41	26.5
Centre Party	196 005	8.6	12	7.7
Christian Democrats	274 516	12.1	22	14.1
Others	181 324	8.0	2	1.3
Total	2 268 614	99.9	155	99.9

The Parliament building (The Storting) is centrally positioned in Oslo.

The three most recent Prime Ministers: Left to right: Lars Korvald (1972-1973), Trygve Bratteli (1973-1976), Odvar Nordli (1976-).

Composition of Parliament:

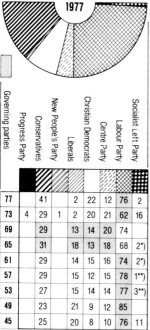

	Progress Party	Conservatives	New People's Party	Liberals	Christian Democrats	Centre Party	Labour Party	Socialist Left Party
77		41			2	22	12	76	2
73	4	29	1		2	20	21	62	16
69		29		13	14	20	74	
65		31		18	13	18	68	2*)
61		29		14	15	16	74	2*)
57		29		15	12	15	78	1**)
53		27		15	14	14	77	3**)
49		23		21	9	12	85	
45		25		20	8	10	76	11

(Governing parties indicated at far left bracket)

*)The Socialist People's Party
**)The Communist Party

The figures show the apportionment of seats in the Storting in respect of parties. Left column: Election year.

support in the Storting from the Socialist Left Party in a number of matters, and from one or more non-socialist party in other matters, especially in connection with foreign affairs.

The appointment of Storting representatives is undertaken on a county basis, and each party is organised into its own county association. If a party gains greater support in the peripheral counties than the more geographically central ones, it might also gain a stronger degree of representation at the Storting than a purely mathematical apportionment of seats in relation to votes would indicate.

THE GOVERNMENT

The Government is dependent upon the majority of the Storting, and it is compelled to carry out its functions by means of the help of the permanent employees of the bureaucracy. The Government, however, will still be able to exert considerable influence on the general course of events through its day to day operations.

The head of the Government is the Prime Minister, and the next after him in rank is considered to be the Foreign Minister. The Prime

GOVERNMENT

Minister's primary role is that of coordinating the functions of the Cabinet Ministers, drawing up the basic policy lines and ensure that these are followed. In connection with the present day's intense international involvement, he also represents the country to a considerable extent, in addition to the Foreign Minister. Among other things, the Premiers of the Nordic countries meet from time to time to consider questions of common interest. The Prime Minister is also a central figure in connection with the Government's contact with officialdom, in that he, inter alia, gives press conferences where he issues statements and where the representatives of the Press are able to question him.

The Cabinet normally meets in the King's presence every Friday. In addition there are informal meetings between the Government members, preferably a couple of times a week. Matters are discussed at these meetings which, among other things, require inter-departmental co-operation in order to carry them out. Such matters have increased in number during recent years, by virtue of the State having assumed increasingly heavier tasks and responsibilities, and the various spheres of social life have become increasingly dependent upon each other.

The Government Departments

The Departments number 14 and are listed here in alphabetical order:
Ministry of Agriculture
Ministry of Church and Education
Ministry of Commerce
Ministry of Communications
Ministry of Consumer Affairs and Government Administration
Ministry of Defence
Ministry of Environment

Ministry of Foreign Affairs
Ministry of Finance
Ministry of Fisheries
Ministry of Industry
Ministry of Justice
Ministry of Local Government and Labour
Ministry of Social Affairs

The Government's activities in the various departments involve economic outlay for the State at any given time. The Ministry of Finance has, as its area of responsibility, the economy of the whole State, which places it in a very central position. The annual budget proposals for each of the Ministries are coordinated by the Ministry of Finance before they are submitted to the Storting. The further preparatory work is there carried out by the Finance Commitee, in the same way that other matters are prepared by the respective standing committees of the Storting.

In addition to the heads of the 14 Ministries, a special Cabinet Post was created in January 1976 in respect of Law of the Sea and Fishing Limit Questions. He has the assistance of a small staff, but no individual Ministry.

Each Minister has an Undersecretary which is a political appointment and means that the incumbent is replaced with a change of government. Otherwise the Ministries are staffed by professional civil servants who serve the successive governments.

COUNTY AND MUNICIPAL ADMINISTRATION

Norway is divided into 19 counties. Among these, the capital, Oslo, constitutes a separate county, which is also the most heavily populated with c. 450 000 inhabitants, or more than 10 per cent of the country's total population of c. 4 millions. The smallest number of inhabitants is recorded by the county of Finnmark, far north of the Polar Circle, with c. 80 000. But, on the other hand, it has the greatest area of all the counties. Apart from the capital, all the counties include both urban and rural communities.

The counties constitute administrative units between the State and the individual municipalities with regard to the undertaking of tasks which are reasonably expected to be accomplished jointly. This is particularly true of hospital administration and other health services, education, communications and certain other things such as supply of electricity to the municipalities which are included in the county.

The Storting has issued legislation which provides for certain tasks to be undertaken by all the counties, while other measures are implemented by individual counties working on their own initiative.

The county is governed by a popularly elected assembly, the County Council, with its own county administration. Direct election to the County Councils was first held in the Autumn of 1975, in conjunction with the local municipal elections.

Urban and Rural Municipalities

Norway consists of c. 450 municipalities. Of these, c. 50 are urban municipalities while the rest are rural ones. The second largest town, after the capital, is Bergen with something in excess of 200 000 inhabitants, after which comes Trondheim with just under 150 000.

Each municipality is governed by a popularly elected Municipal Council. All municipalities deal with church and education questions, social and health services, building and fireservice questions, communications and a number of other matters.

A number of municipalities have been merged during the last couple of decades, because larger administrative units were desired. But a certain trend in the opposite direction is also discernible; a number of matters in large municipalities such as the capital have been transferred to individual suburban committees.

DOMESTIC POLICIES

Norwegian domestic policies after the second world war have mainly concentrated on economic matters, not least of all on the question of what role the State should play in the nation's economic life.

On the two sides of the delineation socialist/non-socialist, there are different opinions as to what extent private initiative and private ownership should be allowed to function. Another important theme of the political debate is the question of what advantages and disadvantages are inherent in the on-going industrialisation and urbanisation of the Norwegian society. The new element which was introduced into Norwegian social life by virtue of the large discoveries of oil and gas in the North Sea in the 1960's, has also created a wide-ranging debate on the role of the State in this development, and there has been some disagreement as to the extent to which private companies should be allowed to participate in this exploitation besides the State. There is, furthermore, disagreement as to how quickly such exploitation should take place. A high exploitation tempo is thought to offer advantages to industry, but it is feared that it may also involve environmental disadvantages and injurious effects for older industries, such as fishing along the coast.

A long list of individual matters affecting Norwegian domestic policies could be quoted from recent years. In the non-economic field questions of education have featured predominantly, inter alia with regard to the marking system at schools, as has the question of abortion legislation and the control of sales of alcohol and tobacco. As far as economic matters are concerned, tax levels have featured the most. However, it often seems unrealistic to delineate between domestic and foreign political questions. Many matters, both economic. e.g. in connection with oil exploitation and fishing, and non-economic, e.g. in connection with the abuse of drugs, require a collective judgement where conditions and circumstances both within and outside Norway's territory, are taken into account.

Foreign and National Security Policies

Norwegian foreign policy is determined by the country's geographical situation, its political and economic interests, as well as the will to defend the way of life and the type of society which has been developed during the country's long history.

Norwegian foreign policy debates are characterised by the desire of the people to live in peace and friendly cooperation with others. Each Norwegian government has to take this into consideration. Besides wide-ranging cultural contacts, this peace promoting activity is strengthened through extensive foreign trade and shipping. At the same time Norway has reacted against every form of oppression of other peoples and ethnic groups all over the world. Protection of human rights and the democratic ideals are central themes of Norwegian foreign policy.

There has at all times been wide political agreement in respect of the main aims of foreign policy. One exception to this was the lengthy debate which arose in connection with the question of which forms Norwegian relations with the European Economic Community should take. The final decision on the matter was taken following an advisory referendum in 1972 which resulted in a narrow majority against Norwegian membership. (53.49% against, 46.51% in favour).

The cooperation between the Nordic countries takes a great number of different forms. In addition to the official co-operative instances, of which the Nordic Council is the most important, a network of informal contacts has been developed during the postwar years, which join the people of the Nordic countries together in the vast majority of spheres; apart from those purely concerned with national security.

Norway and the UN

Norway, as one of the «united nations», took part in the estab-

Trygve Lie, the first Secretary General of the UN.

lishment of the world organisation in 1944—45. Norway's Foreign Minister, Trygve Lie, was the first Secretary General of the UN, and several Norwegians held leading positions among the international staff. Membership has had considerable significance for Norwegian foreign policy. Successive Norwegian governments have emphasised their loyal support of the world organisation's activities and there has been little dissension in Norwegian opinion about the significance of the work of the UN. Norway has fulfilled the responsibilities which are inherent in membership in a conscientious manner. Military units have been placed at the disposal of the UN peace-keeping operations on several occasions. Norwegian officers have served as cease-fire observers in the service of the UN for many years.

There is a comprehensive information service about the UN in operation in Norway, inter alia in all schools. Norwegian authorities have placed great importance on the UN organisation's long-term projects for peace, economic and social development, environmental protection, health, culture and human rights. A fundamental task for the UN is to act as a forum for the debate between the industrialised countries and the developing countries. Norway takes an active part in this debate.

Development Aid

Norway has been engaged in development aid since the middle of the 1950's, and the extent of this activity is gradually increasing. The statistics show that Norway is one of the countries which transfers most — in relation to the gross national product — to development purposes. Half of the Norwegian grants are channelled through multilateral organisations, while the other half is used in conjunction with bilateral projects. Political conditions have never been attached to the use of Norwegian development aid grants. Nor has it been a requirement that these resources are to be used in such a way that they are to the advantage of Norwegian production. So far the Norwegian industrial concerns and financial institutions have only participated in development projects to a modest degree, but the conditions for such an involvment are now being improved. Norwegian aid is directed, first and foremost, at different parts of the infrastructure of the recipient country; lines of communications, harbour installations, production of energy, agriculture and education. For a number of years East-African countries have received a considerable proportion of this bilateral aid. Such aid is now being directed, to an increasing extent, towards Asian countries. Norwegian experts are attached to UN projects in countries throughout the world; many of them in leading positions. Several fishing development programmes in particular have been able to avail themselves of Norwegian experts.

The bilateral aid programme in Norway is administered by the Norwegian Agency for International Development (NORAD), which is under the immediate control of the Foreign Ministry. Multilateral aid is coordinated and the general guidelines decided upon, by a special department for development problems within the Foreign Ministry. It is the Storting which decides upon the extent and contents of Norwegian development aid. An intensive information campaign is being conducted in Norway, illustrating the necessity of giving aid to the developing countries.

Norway actively supports the plans for a «new international economic order» and is willing to accept obligations which will contribute to a more just relationship between the poor and the rich nations. There is particular emphasis placed on giving assistance to the very poorest.

NATO

In 1948 Norway had to renounce the alliance-free policy which had been launched at the end of the second world war. Negotiations were conducted with Denmark and Sweden with regards to a Nordic defence cooperation. When these proved fruitless the Storting resolved that Norway should participate in negotiatons aimed at membership of the Atlantic Treaty. Foreign Minister Halvard Lange signed the treaty on behalf of Norway on April 4, 1949. Membership of the Atlantic Treaty and NATO has subsequently constituted the basis of Norwegian national security policy. This is a course which has enjoyed wide support among the population. The opinion

polls show that, in the 1970's, there was only 6—8 per cent of all Norwegians over the age of 15 who felt that membership of NATO could increase the risk of war for the country. Since Norway is a relatively thinly populated country, involving long distances and with a vulnerable situation, national security is dependent upon cooperation with other states. Part of Norway's role in the common defence involves the development of military sites which receive and supply reinforcements in the event of an international crisis. Allied joint exercises also take place on Norwegian territory, as part of a programme of preparedness.

The defence costs, expressed as a percentage of the gross national product, have varied between 3.3 and 2.8 per cent during the 1970's. It is expected that the figure will fall to 2.5 per cent in the coming years, provided nothing unexpected occurs.

Norway has certain self-imposed restrictions in respect of its national security policy. For example there are no foreign forces stationed in the country during times of peace — with the exception of personnel who are attached to the NATO Northern Command at Kolsås outside Oslo. Several Government declarations have confirmed that a change can only be considered if the country is subjected to attack or threats of attack. The Storting has also resolved that nuclear weapons may not be stationed in Norway — unless the situation should make this an absolute necessity. In such a case the Storting would have to reconsider the matter. Generally speaking it may be said that emphasis is placed on the avoidance by Norway of any step which might be interpreted as a provocation towards any of the states which have common frontiers with the country.

The increased significance of

the northern areas during recent years — a significance which everybody expects to be maintained — makes it important to develop an effective and modern reconnaissance service at sea and in the air. A naval force is to be built up which will have the protection of rights and natural resources as its main function. A coastguard service is expected to be built up at the beginning of the 1980's. Norwegian authorities are extremely concerned with the many tasks which are connected with the Arctic part of the country.

The Continental Shelf

The extent of the Norwegian continental shelf was defined by the Government in 1963 and is built on the so-called exploitation criterion which is also used by many other states. According to the rules which apply to the continental shelf, it is the coastal state which enjoys the exclusive right to the exploitation of, and research into, natural resources on the seabed. The physical limitation of the continental shelf is decided upon as a result of agreements which Norway has with other states.

The Economic Zone

In keeping with the majority of other coastal states, Norway has established an economic zone. This decision became effective from January 1, 1977. It secures for the country the right to the natural resources within the zone — both living resources such as fish and prawns, and mineral resources such as oil and gas. As a general rule the zone extends 200 nautical miles from the territorial limit, but it can extend even further where the continental shelf exceeds that distance.

The reason why Norway has been so strongly in favour of the establishment of an economic zone, is particularly due to the fact that it has been considered necessary to intervene in order to prevent over-fishing in the area. The Norwegian authorities will initiate measures to prevent the extinction of fish species, and the only way that this may be achieved is through the limitation of catches.

Norway has a special minister who is concerned with Law-of-the-Sea matters. The problems which obtain affect several ministerial departments, first and foremost the Ministry of Foreign Affairs, the Ministry of Fisheries, the Ministry of the Environment and the Ministry of Justice.

Oil and Gas

The oil activity on the Norwegian continental shelf plays an important role, both economically, politically, technologically and scientifically. Considerable sums have been invested in this activity besides those sectors of industry which are connected with oil exploration. It is estimated that about 100 billion kroner will be invested up to 1980. Export income from crude oil and the building of drilling rigs began to have a substantial statistical impact in 1975. Part of the oil production in the North Sea is transported to Scotland via pipelines which were brought into operation in October 1975. Gas pipelines lead to Emden in North Germany.

Extraction has, to date, only taken place south of 62°N, but exploratory drilling will soon take place further northwards along the coast as well.

It is quite clear that Norway will receive considerable income from her petroleum resources. Some of the discoveries which have been made are among the richest which have hitherto been found on the seabed.

The Courts of Law

According to the Constitution, Norwegian courts are independent of the other Powers of the State in exercising their adjudicatory functions. Norwegian judges are jurists and senior officeholders who can only be dismissed from their posts by a court judgment.

The ordinary courts of law consist of the Supreme Court, 5 Courts of Appeal, 100 District and City Courts and around 450 Conciliation Boards. There are also special courts for certain kinds of cases, for example the Labour Disputes Courts, the Guardianship Courts, the Land Apportionment Courts and the Fishery Courts.

The fundamental principles of Norwegian court procedure are that cases must be dealt with orally in open court and be decided on the basis of information adduced directly before the adjudicating court. Furthermore, the litigants shall be entitled to acquaint themselves with the statements and evidence to be produced by the other party and shall have the right to contest these. The administration of penal law is based on the principle of indictment. This means that the prosecuting authorities are responsible for producing the necessary evidence in a penal case.

The Supreme Court

has its seat in Oslo. It consists of a Chief Justice and 17 Justices. Each case is heard by 5 Justices. The Justices of the Supreme Court have great influence on court practice. It is therefore the rule that, if there is any question of departing from a concept of the law previously expressed by the Supreme Court, the case must be dealt with in plenary session with all Justices present.

The procedure is oral, but all evidence, including the statements by the parties concerned, must be in writing and submitted by the respective counsel. The Appeals Selection Committee of the Supreme Court, composed of 3 Justices of the Supreme Court, determines whether appeals from lower instances shall be allowed. The Appeals Selection Committee itself may decide appeals relating to certain procedural errors.

The Courts of Appeals

Norway is divided into 5 Court of Appeals jurisdictions, each with its own Court of Appeals. In civil cases, the Court of Appeals is the appeals instance for judgments rendered by the District or City Court. In penal cases, serious felonies are dealt with by the Court of Appeals as the first instance, while less serious offences are dealt with first in the District or City Court, before subsequently, as the case may be, being submitted to the Court of Appeals for a rehearing. All cases are heard by 3 professional judges (jurists). In some civil cases, either 2 or 4 lay judges may be called in to participate in the adjudication process. In penal cases the question of guilt is decided by a jury consisting of 10 lay members, while the sentence is decided by the 3 professional judges.

District and City Courts

At the District and City Courts, penal cases are heard by one judge in cases where there is an unreserved confession (Examining and Summary Court) and otherwise by one judge and two lay judges. In most civil cases the decision is made by one pro-

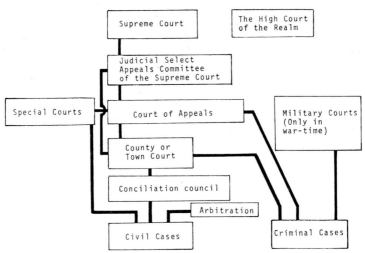

The principal features of the Norwegian legal system

fessional judge, but in certain circumstances lay judges may also be called in.

Conciliation Board

There are Conciliation Boards in each municipality. They consist of 3 members, usually not lawyers, chosen by the municipal council for a period of 4 years. Most civil cases must have been submitted to the Conciliation Board before they may be brought before the courts. The primary objective here is to bring about a settlement between the parties. In certain circumstances the Conciliation Board may pronounce judgment. This is particularly practical in debt cases where the defendant fails to appear. The parties are not permitted to be represented by or appear with a lawyer.

The Labour Disputes Court. Local Labour Courts

The Labour Dispute Court has its seat in Oslo and consists of a president, 2 neutral members and 4 members appointed at the recommendation of the employers' associations and trade unions. The president and one member must be jurists. The Labour Disputes Court deals with disputes concerning wage settlement agreements.

From 1977 onwards certain District and City Courts are designated to act as local Labour Courts in each county. Cases are heard by the judge and two lay judges, some of whom are designated on the recommendation of the employers' associations and trade unions. The local Labour Courts, inter alia, deal with questions relating to dismissal.

The Public Prosecution Authority and the Police

The Public Prosecution Authority is headed by the Director General of Public Prosecutions and 16 State Advocates. In cases involving imprisonment and concerning felonies, the defence is paid by the State.

A special characteristic of the Norwegian judicial system is that senior police officials also belong to the Public Prosecution Authority. In cases concerning misdemeanours of a less serious nature, where the Public Prosecution Authority regards a fine as a suitable punishment, it may issue a writ of optional fine. If this is accepted, the writ of optional fine will have the same effect as a court judgment, and the case will not be brought before the courts. If not accepted, the case will come up in the usual manner. Most writs of optional fine are accepted by the person charged.

The treatment of offenders

In Norway, capital punishment has been abolished for all offences except for the most serious war crimes in war time. The usual punishments are imprisonment and fines. Conditional prison sentences are often applied in respect of juvenile offenders and first-time offenders.

The cost of building and running the prisons is met by the State.

Defence

The main task of the Norwegian defence is to maintain the peace — with freedom intact.

Norway's geographical situation provides the country with a common frontier with the Soviet Union in the north and good opportunities for observing the movements of the Soviet navy from the bases in the Kola area to the vital lines of communication between USA/Canada and Western Europe in the Norwegian Sea and the North Atlantic. Norwegian airspace in the north is in the path of the shortest missile routes between Russia an the USA.

These are factors which have to be taken into consideration with regard to Norwegian defence and national security policies. At the same time there must be no doubt whatever that the country would react violently towards anyone guilty of an incursion into Norwegian territory.

The country's defence has a solid basis in the population. There is no debate worth mentioning in the Storting on the subject of the constitutional compulsory military service which is imposed upon young men for 12—15 months' initial service in peacetime. Women are excused military service, but may opt for voluntary officer training and appointment as professional officers. The country's military forces in peacetime amount to nearly 40 000 men. As a result of the compulsory military training system, Norway would be able to mobilise nearly 300 000 armed men in a war situation.

As a result of Norway's membership of NATO, exercises take place from time to time in the country with participation by other NATO-countries' forces. A limited part of the British forces which are «earmarked» for operations in Norway in the event of war undergo a few weeks' winter training every year in West Norway and in North Norway, in order to equip themselves for this task.

Parts of the air defences are integrated into the NATO air defence system. One or two naval vessels are periodicallly part of STANAVFORLANT and are then under NATO command. The entire Norwegian forces are otherwise under national command in peacetime. The country is divided operationally into Defence Command South Norway and Defence Command North Norway, both of which

A Coastguard vessel inspecting the 200 nautical mile economic zone.

come under the Defence Central Command which, under the leadership of the Commander-in-Chief Defence is located at Huseby in Oslo.

In a crisis/war situation the Government is empowered to transfer command of the Norwegian forces to the Commander-in-Chief of the NATO Northern Command which has its headquarters at Kolsås near Oslo. He wil exercise his command through the commanding officers of the two operational area commands, to which allied forces who come to the country's assistance may be seconded. In the event of such a transfer of command, the Commander-in-Chief Defence becomes an advisor to the Government. The Norwegian Government has decided, voluntarily and unilaterally, that foreign troops are not to be stationed on Norwegian territory during times of peace, and that no atomic weapons are to be stored on Norwegian soil.

THE ARMY

The army is apportioned c. 65% of the annual call-up of about 25 000 men. The largest unit is the North Norway Brigade (Troms)

which numbers about 5 000 men. Otherwise there are large garrisons in Porsanger and West-Finnmark and in South-Varanger by the Norwegian—Russian frontier. The recruit schools (3—6 months' basic training) are situated in South Norway where, apart from HM the King's Guard (c. 600 men), there are only a few small standing army units. The reason for this disposition is that the attack routes directed against South Norway are covered by the country's NATO allies Denmark and West Germany, while in the north Norway is alone in the front line of the NATO Alliance.

NAVAL DEFENCES

The naval defences (19% of the total call-up) consist of the Navy and the Coastal Artillery. The naval vessels have their main bases at Haakonsvern, Olavsvern (in Bergen and Tromsø) and Ramsund warship depots. The submarines and the fast torpedo/gunboats are specially constructed for the Norwegian coastal waters. The TKB's, frigates and corvettes are equipped with Norwegian-produced missile systems. The

Coastal Artillery has been issued with new fire-guidance equipment and watches over key points along the coast from a number of emplacements built into the rock.

The Coastguard

The Coastguard is a special part of the Naval Defences with responsibility for the supervision and inspection of the 200 nautical mile economic zone which was introduced in 1977. For the time being the Navy carries out this duty with the 12 fishery protection vessels which were responsible for the old 12-mile fishing limit. Seven specially constructed Coastguard vessels have been designed and ordered however, with delivery expected around 1980. The Air Force's P-3B Orion and C-130 Hercules aircraft also undertake inspection operations in the 200-mile zone.

THE AIR DEFENCES

The Air Defences consist of the Air Force, Anti-aircraft defences and the Inspection and Early Warning Service. It is intended that the Air Force be equipped with 72 new F16 aircraft during the 1980's. At present it possesses the following fighter/fighter-bomber aircraft: F-104 G Starfighters, CF 104 and F-5A Freedom Fighters, besides, inter alia, RF-5A photo-reconnaissance aircraft, maritime reconnaissance P-3B Orions and C-130 Hercules transports. The Air Rescue Service with Sea King helicopters is also assisted by the Air Defences.

The anti-aircraft defences in the central eastern area around Oslo are equipped with a batallion of Nike Hercules anti-aircraft missiles. Short-range defence of airfields will be catered for by the supply of Roland II missiles.

The Inspection and Early Warning Service consists of radar stations which cover Norwegian airspace and which, by means of electronic computers, watch, warn and calculate the operational possibilities of retaliatory action against threats from the air against Norwegian territory.

The Home Guard

The Home Guard has a mobilisation strength of c. 80 000 men who may be called to arms within a few hours. The compulsory service amounts to 50 hours a year. The majority of the Home Guard soldiers cover preparedness tasks for the Army and other land forces, while the Naval Home Guard and the Air Defence Home Guard perform the same functions for the Naval Defences and the Air defences respectively.

Finance

FINANCE AND MONEY POLICIES

The Government tries to a greater or lesser extent to controle or influence economic development by means of its economic policy. Finance polioy and money- and credit policies are of great significance with regard to economic policies, especially in respect of the influence of the extent of private and official demand. ·

Finance policy covers:
— the official purchases of goods and services
— the taxation of income and capital
— social security grants and other grants to private interests and abroad
— subsidies and duties.

During the 1970's the trade organisations and the State have agreed on a so-called comprehensive incomes settlement, wherein, inter alia, taxation policy is developed in direct association with the nominal increase in income. The finance policy may thereby be said to be integrated in the price- and incomes policy.

A principle objective of the money- and credit policies is to control the extent of the combined credit flow. This is achieved by regulating the loan volume by the different types of credit institutions. For example, the loan volume from the commercial and saving banks is regulated by the banks being required to place a certain part of their available capital as a deposit with the Bank of Norway (the central bank) and in national treasury bills of exchange, and through the requirement to place a certain proportion of the increased available capital in bonds. The loan volume is regulated by the employment of varying interest rates.

The State banks are directly under the control of the Government.

With regard to the bond market, the offers, demand and loan conditions are controlled by the authorities. The offer is controlled through the Ministry of Finance having to issue permission for the floating of a bond loan, and the demand for bonds is ensured through the requirement, inter alia, that life insurance companies, commercial banks and savings banks purchase bonds for a specific part of the growth in their available capital.

A number of interest rates are agreed as a result of negotiations between the authorities and the private finance institutions. The interest rates for the State banks' loans are determined directly by the authorities.

OFFICIAL FINANCES

Government Revenue and Expenditure

The official sector consists of the State, the county municipalities and the primary municipalities. The most important functions of the municipalities are to be found in the areas of education, health, social welfare and communication.

The most important functions of the State lie on the traditional national level where the economic policy is determined, and otherwise with regard to the areas of defence, research and higher education, communications, health service, social security and the judicial system.

The main part of Government revenue is derived from taxation (table 1, p. 28). Only a minor part derives from capital income, i.e. income from interest and dividends from Government-administered business. The table does not include income from the **State** concerns.

Direct taxation and social security contributions form the largest source of income. Of direct taxation, about $2/3$ goes to the municipalities. The State's most important sources of income are through indirect taxation, wherein are included first and foremost value added tax and investment tax.

On the expenditure side, about half of the revenue is transferred to the consumers in the form of pensions, price reductions on goods and services, and other forms of support. In this way only about half of the tax revenue is put into use with State-administered concerns and investments.

Table 1. The official administration's revenue and expenditure. Million kroner 1976.

Revenue

Capital revenue	4 227
Direct taxes and social security contributions ..	50 065
Indirect taxation	31 165
Total revenue	85 457

Expenditure

Interest	4 167
Social security and other support to private consumers	28 028
Subsidies	11 378
Foreign grants	1 084
Official consumption	29 137
Capital growth	11 663
Total expenditure	85 457

TAXES

The primary objective of taxation is to:
— provide revenue for State administration and investments
— influence the apportionment of revenue and capital
— influence the development of production, employment and prices.

The most important element of the tax system is the direct personal incomes tax. Table 2 shows the total income tax expressed as a percentage of the gross income, where no heed has been taken of special tax concessions which many people are entitled to in respect of loan interest, travelling expenses, care of children, etc. Income tax includes municipal taxes, contributions to social security, and a state tax with sliding scale of percentage deduction in relation to increased income level.

The income tax has a ceiling of 73 per cent of gross income. The maximum tax differential is 73%. A person with a considerable capital wealth and a modest income, may pay up to 90 per cent of his income in tax, however, when income and capital tax is added together.

Limited companies pay income tax of up to 51 per cent of net income.

All employers must also pay between 12.3—16.5 per cent of paid wages to the social security.

In addition, there is tax paid on capital and inheritance, but this only results in modest income to the official instances.

Table 2. Tax as a percentage of income in 1977

Gross income	Class 1[1])	Class 2[2])
40 000	24.8	19.7
60 000	30.2	24.4
80 000	35.2	28.8
100 000	40.4	33.3
150 000	50.1	44.1

[1]) People who are assessed individually
[2]) Married couples with one major source of income

Another important element of the taxation system is the purchase taxes. The most important of these is the value added tax of 20 per cent of the processing value on most goods and services. A number of goods and services are wholly, or partially, free of this tax, including health services, books and public transport. Other goods, which include cars, alcohol and tobacco, are subject to additional duties. Goods and services which are directed at investment purposes are subject to a tax of only 13 per cent.

The sales of a number of goods are subsidised. This is first of all true in the case of foodstuffs and public transport via bus, train or ship.

Social Security Expenditure Per Capita in Norway 1968–1973

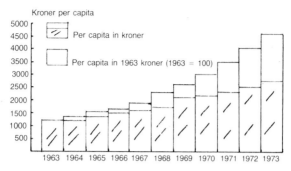

Per capita expenditure for social services have more than tripled in the period 1963—1973. Even after allowance has been made for monetary depreciation, outlays for such services have been doubled.

An often used indicator of the total taxation burden in a country is the total amount of tax expressed as a percentage of the gross national product. This may also be expressed as a net figure by the gross tax amounts being reduced by the figure which equals transfers to the private sector. In this way one is afforded an expression of how great a part of the created wealth is used by the official instances in connection with administration and investments.

Table 3. Gross and net taxation in certain countries expressed as a percentage of the gross national product in 1974.

	Gross taxes	Net taxes
The Netherlands ..	47.1	21.7
Norway	46.3	24.8
Denmark	45.7	30.9
Sweden	44.7	26.8
West Germany ...	39.1	23.5
France	37.5	17.9
United Kingdom ..	36.9	22.4
Canada	34.1	22.7

SOCIAL SECURITY

Support is given via social security in the event of, inter alia, reaching retirement age at 67 years, disability, sickness and unemployment. All are, in principle, entitled to assistance through social security.

Having reached 67 years of age, or having become disabled, a pension is paid which varies according to income during the insured person's active working life. Everyone is, however, guaranteed a tax-free minimum pension which, in 1977, amounts to 17 661 kroner for single people and 28 156 kroner for married couples. For the purpose of comparison, it may be pointed out that the average income for a male industrial worker in 1977 is estimated as being c. 65 000 kroner.

THE CREDIT MARKET

Credit Flow

In 1976 the credit flow to the private sector and the municipalities totalled 40 billion kroner. Of this figure, 15 billion kroner took the form of net capital loans from abroad and 25 billion kroner constituted credit flow from domestic sources.

The Bank of Norway

The Bank of Norway (Norges Bank) is the country's central bank. It is organised as a limited company and the State owns all the shares. The bank carries out the functions which a central bank normally undertakes, and is only involved in normal banking activities to a modest degree. The Bank of Norway presents its proposals to the Finance Department as to how the Government's money- and credit policies may best be carried out in practice. The Bank has a monopoly with regard to the issuing of notes and coin in Norway.

The main office of the Bank of Norway is in Oslo, with 20 branches throughout the country.

The State Banks

The State Banks play an important role in the credit market. They have been created in order to ensure a reasonable credit availability for special objectives which the authorities have given high priority to on social, commercial or regional grounds. There are 10 State banks altogether. The Housing Bank is the largest and finances about 75 per cent of house building. In 1976 the credit flow from the State banks was 7.5 billion kroner, and of this figure, 3.1 billion came from the Housing Bank. The Post Office Savings Bank is the only one of the State banks which finances its loans through deposits. The credit flow from the Post Office Savings Bank was nearly 0.3 billion kroner in 1976. All the other instances finance their activities either through loans from the State or by the issuing of bonds which the State guarantees.

The Savings Banks

The Savings Banks have long traditions in Norway. The first savings bank was established in 1822. At the end of 1976 there were 368 savings banks, and their total available capital amounted to 39 billion kroner. The majority of the savings banks are closely connected to their local environment. The banks play an important role as the recipients and administrators of the small savers' money. The savings banks are self-owning institutions without private ownership interests. They conduct normal banking business and are important financing sources for the housing market. About half of their total loans are made up of housing loans. The savings banks grant mainly medium and long-term mortgage loans, but also ordinary commercial loans to trade and industry.

The Commercial Banks

The Commercial Banks are organised as limited companies. By the end of 1976 there were 27 commercial banks, and their combined available capital amounted to 52 billion kroner. The commercial banks are connected to their local environment to a far lesser extent than the savings banks, and the largest of them have branches throughout the whole country. The available capital of the three largest banks (Den norske Creditbank, Bergen Bank and Christiania Bank og Kreditkasse) amounts to almost 30 billion kroner, or about 57 per cent of the combined available capital of the commercial banks. The most important customers of the commercial banks are trade and industry. The close connections with trade and industry become apparent if one considers the apportionment of deposit and loan. About 28 per cent of the total amount lent takes the form of credit and about 26 per cent of deposits made by the public are deposits on demand.

Insurance

There are 12 Life Insurance Companies and their combined available capital amounts to about 20 billion kroner. Half of the increase in this capital has to be placed in bonds. The other loans are primarily directed at commerce and housing.

There are 25 company units within casualty insurance which work together on a nationwide basis. In addition there are a number of smaller companies which operate on a local basis. The combined available capital of the casualty insurance companies amounts to about 9 billion kroner. The companies are not required to place funds with bearer bonds, but the volume of loans to the private and municipal sectors is controlled directly by the authorities.

Credit Undertakings

Credit undertakings are credit institutions which gain access to their financial means via taking up bond loans. There are altogether 15 credit undertakings, and they are largely directed at specific objectives, businesses and districts with regard to long-term credit. Their credit flow in 1976 was about 2.7 billion kroner.

There are also a number of **private financing companies.** The individual company is able to pursue one or more types of activity. Some are engaged in activities which are closely related to normal banking, while others have specialised in a specific type of financing. There are thus special institutions within the area of hire purchase, factoring, leasing and credit cards.

Economy

GENERAL SURVEY

Norway is the first Western industrialised country which has become a net exporter of oil. The aim of the moderate, long-term extraction policy is an annual production of c. 90 million tons of oil equivalents (toe). This is 5 times more than Norway's total energy consumption in 1976 — and 10 times the consumption of petroleum products. With an annual production of c. 75 million toe on the average during the 1980's, the State will receive an revenue of c. 20 billion kroner. It was expected that the gross national product would amount to close on 200 billion kroner in 1977. The anticipated large incomes from the oil and gas discoveries in the North Sea have enabled Norway to borrow tens of billions of kroner from abroad, partly with a view to maintaining high employment during the recession and particularly with a view to investment in petroleum activities.

The accumulated foreign trade deficit amounted to c. 50 billion kroner in 1976. The debt per capita was c. 12 500 kroner. But the main amounts applied to the private sector — the State was responsible for only a minor part. The State loans, with an average 30 years repayment schedule, will amount to barely one half billion kroner a year.

Of the annual income from petroleum of c. 20 billion kroner in the 1980's, only about 5 billion will be able to be used domestically. Too large infusions of capital can bring about too much inflationary pressure and a too rapid structural alteration to commercial life. In addition it should be possible to invest c. 10 billion annually in petroleum activities. The remaining 5 billion per year will be exported,

Share of GNP and Employment

	Billion kr. 1976	%1976	%1950	Work years 1976	%1976	%1950
Forestry	1.9	1.2	2.6	10 000	0.6	2.2
Agriculture	6.2	3.6	7.5	113 000	7	23.8
Fishing, whaling	1.8	1.1	3.7	21 000	1.3	3.7
Industry, mining	36.4	21.4	27.5	399 000	24.7	24.2
Power supply	5.7	3.4	2.1	16 000	1	0.8
Oil extraction	6.4	3.8	—	2 000	0.1	—
Building, sites	13	7.6	6.6	139 000	8.6	7.3
Retail trade	33	19.4	15.2	213 000	13.2	8.9
Shipping	8.2	4.8	11.1	47 000	2.9	3.9
Other transport	10.7	6.3	5.8	114 000	7	5.5
Other services .. .. .. Off. adm. etc	46.6	27,4	17.9	539 000	33.6	19.6
	170	100	100	1 613 000	100	100

partly through bond investment, and partly through the establishment of Norwegian industries abroad.

In spite of its decisive significance for Norwegian economy, the petroleum industry will never involve more than a couple of per cent of the country's working population of c. 1.8 million. But from being Western Europe's poorest country in the 1920's, Norway was already one of the most industrialised and richest countries even before the advent of the oil-boom. As early as 1970 Norway was among the top ten countries in the world with regard to gross national product on a per capita basis. By 1976, Norway was third, only 10% behind Sweden and Switzerland.

Ordinary industry employs c. 400 000 people and accounts for about $1/4$ of the total of 1.6 million working years in paid employment. In addition there are about 140 000 employed in building and construction, with the development of hydro-electric power as a speciality. Barren mountain areas constitute about $2/3$ of the area of Norway, and these have proved valuable as reservoirs for the hydro-electric development which has been the major force behind Norwegian industry prior to the advent of oil on the scene.

Norway has the world's highest production of electricity per capita, — almost twice as much as the next two countries, Canada and USA. Almost all is hydro-electric power which may be developed further until the 1990's. The annual production is expected to increase from c. 70 billion kilowatt hours in 1974 to c. 95 billion in 1980, and c. 112 billion by 1985.

About 45 per cent of this power goes to particularly high energy-consuming industries, with the electro-metallurgical industry most in mind. Norway is West Europe's biggest producer of aluminium, and fifth largest in the world with an annual production of c. 600 000 tons. Norway also provides 25% of the Western European ferro-alloy requirements, with an annual production amounting to c. 750 000 tons.

The Norwegian economy is very export oriented. The average exports for the years 1971—75 in terms of goods and services, amounted to 43% of the gross national product. About $1/3$ of this is covered by gross incomes from shipping. For over 100 years Norway has been among the top 3—4 shipping nations in the world, and with a merchant fleet of c. 40 million t.dw. at the end of 1976, we occupy a safe 4th place.

The export of goods accounted

Gross National Product 1976

	Billion kr.		Per cent
Private consumption		93.5	55
Official consumption		28.8	17
Civilian	23.5		14
Military	5.3		3
Gross investment		63.6	37.3
Buildings, plants	27		16
Ships	8		4.6
Oil equipment	11.8		6.9
Machinery, cars etc.	15		8.8
Stock changes	1.8		1
Export surplus .. ..'		— 15.9	9.3
Exports	69.2		40.7
÷ Imports	85.1		50
GROSS NATIONAL PRODUCT		170	100

for 29% of the GNP on the average. The export of metals, including semi-finished products, accounts for c. 20%. This share increases to 30% when steel is included, as opposed to the 26% for the machine-shop industry.

But it is the machine-shop industry which has recorded the greatest growth since EFTA, and the subsequent agreements with the EEC have pulled down the tariff barriers for finished goods.

If we examine the ten-year period 1964—73, before oil exports gained any significance, the machine-shop industry increased its share to c. 5.5 billion kroner of a combined industrial goods export of 20.7 billion. The annual growth of the machine-shop industry was nearly 18%, as opposed to 10.6% for all groups of wares.

The primary iron and metal industry, which had a 33% share in 1964, increased by 9.2% annually, so that the share in 1973 amounted to c. 30%.

The wood processing industry, which for a long time was one of Norway's most important export branches of industry, had a 20% share in 1964. But with a bare 5% annual increase this fell to 11% in 1973 — about the same as for the chemical industry. The wood processing industry now has

to import ¼ of its raw materials, primarily from Sweden and Finland.

Fish and fish products maintains its share of c. 5% both with regard to Norwegian goods export and Norway's share of the world's total fishing catch. With year's catches of c. 3 million tons, Norway catches about 750 kilos of fish per inhabitant, while the per capita consumption is about 20 kilos per year on the average.

Norway's gross national product has increased regularly by 4—5 per cent annually during the 1970's. The estimates for 1979—1982 have hovered around 4.5 per cent, with petroleum activities excluded. This should afford an additional c. 3 per cent.

The greatest problem facing the Norwegian economy is rapidly increasing labour costs. In 1976 Sweden alone was ahead, but Norway has gradually caught up. In order to suppress inflation and strengthen Norway's competitiveness in world markets, the authorities and the industrial and commercial organisations have introduced so-called combined price and wage agreements. By means of adjustments to taxes and subsidies, the authorities are able to guarantee an increase in the real, available buying power with lower, nominal wage increases. The problem is that of controlling wage-glide, when employment is constantly high. On an annual basis the unemployment figures in 1976 were less than 1.5 per cent.

The OECD has expressed its fears that Norway's combined agreement — the first of its kind in the world — may be upset by large supplements for agriculture, which has lagged behind in respect of wage increases. But Norwegian industrial and commercial life is characterised by centralised, responsible organisations. Relatively very few working days caused by industrial actions, is one of the main factors behind Norway's strong economic growth after 5 year's occupation and the running down of the productive machinery during the second world war.

The 1 770 000 who are in gainful employment together account for c. 1.6 million working years. Of these, 62% are men, and 38% are women. The female employment percentage is increasing, but is still low by international standards. In the age-groups 16—74, the employment percentage for men was 78, and 48 for women.

Even in 1975, when the majority of industrial countries experienced a decrease in their GNP, that of Norway increased by 3.5 per cent — the highest of the four countries which reported growth. In 1976 Norway's growth was 5.7 per cent, somewhat above the OECD average. A total of 8 per cent was estimated for 1977. Without oil and shipping, the increase was estimated as being 4.5 per cent, the same as for 1976.

THE OIL INDUSTRY

Up to and including 1977 drilling for petroleum on the Norwegian Continental Shelf has only taken place south of the 62 parallel. But in this part of the Norwegian Con-

tinental Shelf alone, the reserves have been calculated as being between 1 and 2 billion tons of oil, and between 1 000 and 2 000 billion cubic metres of gas. This alone would be able to ensure an annual rate of production of 90 million toe for the rest of this century. In addition, there is the Norwegian shelf north of 62°N, with an area five times as great as that which has been exploited to date. Even though it involves somewhat deeper waters with greater technical problems, including climatic ones, the petroleum reserves here are expected to be able to provide an annual production of 90 million toe for at least one hundred years.

The huge foreign oil companies were just about to give up drilling in the Norwegian sector of the North Sea, when the first commercially viable discoveries were made in the Ekofisk field around Christmas in 1969. The first companies applied for drilling permission in 1962 and commenced drilling in 1966.

The Ekofisk area which lies in the south-west corner of the Norwegian sector, will attain an annual production rate of c. 35 million tons of oil and nearly 20 billion cubic metres of gas round about 1980. A pipeline for oil has been laid to Teesside in England, and a gas pipeline to Emden in West Germany. Apart from the original Ekofisk field, petroleum is simultaneously extracted from several smaller finds in the same area, including West Ekofisk, Tor and Cod. The operator is Phillips Petroleum of the USA.

The Frigg field, which is one of the world's largest offshore gasfields, was declared economically exploitable in 1972. It rests on the border between the Norwegian and British sectors, with about 55% on the Norwegian side. All the gas from the Frigg field has been sold to the British Gas Corporation, and

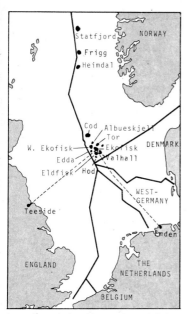

Location of the Norwegian oil-fields in the North Sea.

will be transported via pipeline to St. Fergus in Scotland. The French oil company Elf is the operator for Petronord, which owns the Frigg field, and which has undertaken to transport up to 2.5 billion cubic metres of gas to Karmøy per year, or some other suitable place in the Norwegian coast. The gas will be extracted from a neighbouring field to Frigg.

The pipelines to Norway involve special problems on account of the Norwegian Trench, a 250—500 metre deep subsidence along the Norwegian coast. A pipeline from Frigg would have to negotiate a depth of almost 300 metres, and must have modest dimensions in order to avoid being squashed flat by the pressure of the water. Another problem is the physical consumption of gas in Norway, where there is no pipeline network for gas.

The largest oil discovery which has been made to date in the North Sea was on the Statfjord field. The Norwegian State's oil company, Statoil, has a 50% share in Statfjord through «carried interests». The Norsk Hydro company, in which the State has just over a 50% share, is another major owner of the Statfjord field. Statfjord is expected to be able to provide 30—40 million tons of oil equivalents per year from 1985—87, or almost half of the anticipated total production of the Norwegian sector at that time.

The State's tax incomes from petroleum activities are partly based on production duties, also called royalties. The rates vary according to production, but 11 per cent of the gross sales income is paid on average, based on world market prices.

In addition there are the direct income taxes which, based on a very complicated system, will be payable on about 65 per cent of the profits. The world market prices — which are primarily decided by OPEC — and the rapidly increasing costs of offshore petroleum activities will determine the State's income.

In 1976 the oil price was c. 12 dollars a barrel, while production costs on known Norwegian fields amounted to c. 4 dollars per barrel on average. With a profit margin of 8 dollars per barrel, and a production level of 75 million toe, State income will be about 17 billion kroner a year.

Since drilling permission was given for about 20 per cent of the area south of the 62 parallel, and about 150 wells drilled, some 25 discoveries have been made. Of these about 15 are regarded as being economically viable.

For the ten fields which are expected to be productive in the 1980's, there are proven reserves of 2 245 million tons of oil and 803 billion cubic metres of gas. But with the present-day technology, only 717 million tons of oil and 516 billion cubic metres of gas is extractable, according to calculations made by the State-run Petroleum Directorate.

Critics maintain that the authorities have slowed down the development of the petroleum activity more than was originally estimated, and that it may prove difficult to attain the planned production goals. At least 5—10 years elapse between a discovery being made and extraction commencing. The State income estimates may prove incorrect.

The most immediate problem, however, is the decrease in the amount of deliveries from Norwegian industry to the petroleum activity. Of the c. 25 000 who where employed in petroleum activity in 1976, only a fraction worked out in the North Sea. The vast majority were involved in the construction of platforms or other investments connected with the oil industry, or engaged in supplying services connected with operating the platforms.

The Norwegian company, the Aker Group, which includes most of the larger Norwegian shipyards with a total of 12 000 employees, have become world pioneers where the development and building of semi-submersible drilling rigs are concerned. About 30 of the H-3 type of rig which was developed by the company, have been ordered — more than any other type of platform in the world. Many are built under licence at foreign yards. About half of the Aker Group's employees are engaged in petroleum-oriented activities. The Aker Group has also developed several other types of platform and gigantic buoys for loading tankers on the fields.

A number of smaller ship- and boatyards along the coast, supply the oil industry with supply ships and tugs, and more than 40 such vessels are wholly or partly owned by Norwegian shipping companies.

Norwegian owner interests, shipowners in particular, are behind c. 50 oil-drilling rigs. Both with regard to vessels and drilling rigs, Norwegian companies set their sights at a far wider market than the Norwegian sector of the North Sea, where between 6 and 20 drilling rigs are expected to be in simultaneous activity during the coming 10 years.

The Norwegian building and construction industry has been involved in oil. The Norwegian contracting company, A/S Høyer Ellefsen has made a pioneering contribution with regard to the development and building of large concrete production platforms. The first, Condeep, was towed out to the North Sea and positioned in the British Sector during the summer of 1975. The platform was constructed by Norwegian Contractors, a partnership composed of Norway's leading contractors, and it had a deadweight of c. 200 000 tons. The base section has a storage capacity of 1 million barrels of oil. The platform rests at a depth of 117 metres, and towers 24 metres above the sea. Apart from the economic and installation-wise advantages, the concrete platform is probably the best solution with regard to safe oil extraction at greater depths at present, 300 metres appears to be the limit for such oil production.

In 1974—75 there were c. 30 new orders for production platforms, of which 11 were in concrete, and several new building docks were fitted out in West Norway. A subsequent fall in petroleum activity has, however, led to redundancies at the building yards, so that there are now only about 300 jobs left in this sector.

The greatest decrease in numbers of jobs has been experienced in connection with the building of steel platforms and supply ships. From August 1976

Vøringfoss, at Eidsfjord in Hardanger – one of the biggest and most spectacular waterfalls in Norway.

until the same time the following year, the number of jobs fell by c. 3 500 to 6 700.

Exploration, drilling and production of petroleum employs c. 5 000, and the figures for service bases, transport, catering and administration, are nearly as high. Where the buildings of refineries and petro-chemical industries are concerned, employment has been almost halved to c. 2 000. The total employment connected with petroleum activities was thereby about 20 000 at the beginning of 1977.

Norwegian industry and commerce hope for 40 per cent share of deliveries to the oil activity in the Norwegian sector of the North Sea. So far this share has only amounted to c. 15 per cent.

The development of Statfjord was the largest single project ever undertaken by Norwegian industry. By the summer of 1976 the invest-ments, including pipelines and terminals, were estimated as being c. 33 billion kroner. At the same time the sale of oil and gas was expected to provide an income of between 200 and 300 billion kroner.

POWER SUPPLY

While the oil industry will be a decisive factor in Norway's economic future, another source of energy — hydro-electric power — has been decisive with regard to the economic development Norway has experienced during the last 60—70 years. With an electricity production of almost 20 000 kilowatt hours per capita a year, Norway has been able to build up an effective industry, and simplify the day-to-day functioning of almost every Norwegian home; in a country with a cold climate and very sparse population. Very few families are without electricity and the price has been so low that electric heating is the norm in the home.

The reason for this lies in the fact that $2/3$ of Norway consists of mountains which collect rich precipitation from the prevalent south-westerly winds. The hitherto worthless mountain areas thus assumed great value. Throughout the country it has cost relatively little to build reservoirs and power stations. But the projects have gradually become more expensive, and the last profitable resources will probably be harnessed by the year 2000.

In 1974 the annual capacity was c. 75 billion kilowatt hours — kWh. The undeveloped hydro-electric power was estimated to be about the same. But economic and ecological considerations will reduce these possibilities. Watercourses with a capacity of 15 billion kWh have already been protected.

In 1974 hydro-electric power still accounted for slightly more than 50 per cent of a combined energy consumption of just under 20 million toe. The State produces 30 per cent of the hydro-electric power, private sources account for 20 per cent and municipalities for the balance.

Consumption of electricity, which is still as good as 100 per cent produced via hydro-electric sources, was 69 billion kWh in 1974 — 41 billion for normal consumption and 28 billion for high energy-consuming industries. At the same time about 6 billion kWh was exported to Sweden which has been connected to the Norwegian national grid since 1960. Norway imports Swedish power when its own reservoirs are poorly filled, — but the rate of import has only been about 1/10 of the rate of export.

The Norwegian Watercourse and Electricity Authority, NVE, expects a combined consumption of 94 billion kWh in 1980, 112 in 1985 and 132 in 1990. The hydro-electric power cover is estimated as being 87, 102 and 112 kWh, and an annual import of c. 5 billion kWh is expected, including surplus energy from Denmark. In 1976—77 two 130 km long DC-cables were laid at the bottom of the Skagerrak between Norway and Denmark.

All the same there will be a deficit from the middle of the 1980's which, it is recommended, should be covered by electricity from nuclear power stations. NVE have produced plans for the building of a 900 MW nuclear power station East of the Oslo Fjord in 1984, building similar stations at Trondheim and in Lower Telemark in 1990, and at Bergen and Lista — near the southernmost tip of Norway — in the year 2000.

Norway is particularly well-suited for the building of nuclear power stations in rock, and for solving the cooling water problems. But anti-nuclear power station opinion has forced the Government to concentrate on a temporary plan, where gas-fired power stations replace nuclear power, with an addition of 5 billion kWh in 1985.

The gas in the North Sea contains little sulphur, so that the danger of SO_2-emission is insignificant. But still only about $1/3$ of the energy in gas is able to be converted to electricity. On the other hand Norwegian companies have prepared plans for gas-power stations mounted on floating platforms, with high-tension cables along the seabed to the shore. Such plants may be the only economic solution for exploitation of a number of smaller gas discoveries in the North Sea. The Aker Group has submitted plans for a plant producing 750 MW on a platform with a 41 000 tons displacement.

A heat-energy addition to the Norwegian electricity supply has been desirable for a long time, because it enables greater exploitation of the water resources. The most elastic regulation of electricity supply is afforded by oil-fired stations. Gas-fired stations ashore must be worked continously in order to cover the investments in a pipeline from the gas field to the shore. But both kinds of station, as well as nuclear power, ensure improved employment of the hydro-electric power, by assuming the basic load where it is often too lavish to use the reservoirs, with exceptional possibilities for energy storage.

Where solid fuel is concerned, Norway has had an annual consumption of c. 800 000 tons of coal, of which over $1/3$ is extracted from Spitzbergen. There are no coal deposits in Norway. But since new fields have been discovered at Spitzbergen, containing between 10 and 20 million tons of coal, the annual production can be increased to at least 800 000 tons.

An oil refinery commenced operations at Mongstad, north of Bergen in 1975.

INDUSTRY AND MINING

The incomes from the oil activity will indirectly be partly used for some degree of restructuring Norwegian industry, directed towards a more capital- and know-how demanding production. This is also necessary because of rapidly increasing labour costs and stricter environmental requirements. The principal sources of pollution of water and air are to be removed within ten years. This is expected to consume c. 3 per cent of the annual gross investments in Norwegian industry.

From 1960 to 1970 employment by industry increased by 1 per cent annually, or c. 50 000 work years altogether. At the beginning of the 1970's the annual increase was only 0.3 per cent, and from a total employment of nearly 400 000 work years in the mid-1970's a reduction of 20 000 work years net, is expected up to 1980. In industry which is vulnerable to foreign competition, the decrease will be as much as 35 000, but this will be partly balanced by oil-oriented industries and growth in «protected» industries.

Norwegian industry is still characterised by small units, although there is a clear trend towards concentration. Between 1962 and 1972, the number of firms with less than 5 employees fell from c. 9 200 to 5 500. At the same time, the number of firms with over 200 employees increased from 260 to 300, and the combined number of employees at these larger firms increased from c. 125 000 to 150 000. Over half of the total workforce of 385 000 were employed in firms with at least 100 employees.

Foreign ownership interests are increasing in Norway, but as a whole they are still of a limited nature. From 1963 to 1971 the number of firms with a foreign ownership share of 50 per cent or more, increased from 140 to 184, with a total of 32 600 employees. These firms' share of the total number of employed in industry rose from 6 to 8.5 per cent, and their share of the processing value from 7.6 to 11 per cent. In addition there are 70 companies where the ownership share is between 20 and 49 per cent. These employed a total of 13 750.

The foreign interests are particularly prevalent in the energy-intensive and electro-technical industries.

The State's share in Norwegian industry has increased from 6 to 9 per cent in total, since 1974. But Norway is still among those countries in Western Europe with the lowest proportion of state-ownership. In Austria and France, which are at the top of the list, the state-owned shares are 14 and 13 per cent respectively. The Norwegian State's involvement is concentrated on heavy industry.

The State oil company, Statoil, which had a mere c. 250 employees in 1976, will naturally expand considerably in the coming years. Otherwise the largest companies controlled by the State are: Norsk Jernverk with 4 200 employees, Kongsberg Våpenfabrikk and Raufoss Ammunisjonsfabrikker — both with about 3 000 employees, Horten Verft (shipbuilders) and the mining company Sydvaranger — both with less than 2 000 employees, and Store Norske Spitzbergen Coal Company at Spitzbergen with 700 workers. In addition the State has a 50.75 per cent interest in Norsk Hydro, Norway's leading chemical concern with almost 10 000 employees, and 75 per cent in ÅSV, which has about 7 200 employees.

Norsk Hydro A/S, which is now a Norwegian pioneer in oil extraction and the petro-chemical industry, was founded in 1905 in order to utilise cheap hydro-electric power for the production of artificial fertilisers.

Today Hydro's fertiliser production — enough to feed over 20 million people indirectly — is based on petroleum, while the electrical power is used for production of aluminium and magnesium — which is extracted from sea-water. Hydro is responsible for 15 per cent of the world production of magnesium, a metal which is lighter even than aluminium.

The Norwegian aluminium industry is extensive. A number of large smelting works were built between 1951 and 1966, and the capacity has since been increased to over 700 000 tons a year in 1973. Norway has 6 per cent of the Western world's aluminium production. The leading countries are USA with 37 per cent, Japan with 12 and Canada with 9 per cent.

Norway's aluminium industry is 40 per cent foreign-owned, 44 per cent State-owned, and only 16 per cent under private ownership. The rapid development and the ties with the large, fully integrated international concerns has led to a one-sided concentration on the most energy-intensive process — with less attention to refining. Only $^1/_5$ of the production is processed in Norway.

Since the availability of cheap hydro-electric power has become less, the Norwegian aluminium industry will probably have to concentrate more on refining. But the smelting works will receive certain grants of power in order to undertake necessary rationalisations.

Norway also has a considerable production of ferro-alloys — the largest in Western Europe where ferro-silicon and ferro-siliconmangate are concerned. Export of ferro-alloys amounted to 780 000 tons, to a value of over 1 750 million kroner. The same year the aluminium exports amounted to c. 640 000 tons and 3 200 million kroner, nickel exports of 34 000 tons and 920 million kroner, zinc exports of 63 000 tons and 270 million kroner, while magnesium worth 410 millioner kroner was exported. In addition there is about 1 million tons of raw steel produced in Norway.

The particularly energy-intensive industries use up about 45 per cent of the electric power which is produced, while industry as a whole accounts for c. 60 per cent.

The timber trade was the most important Norwegian export for hundreds of years. Exports of lumber dominated until this century, but then came the advent of wood processing. In spite of a slower rate of growth in recent years because of raw material limitations, wood processing accounted for 7 per cent of the total production value for industry and mining in 1975. In 1976, 650 000 tons of paper pulp was exported at a value of 1 100 million kroner, 380 000 tons of newsprint worth almost 700 million kroner, and 220 000 tons of other paper worth 550 million kroner. Wood processing employed 21 400 in 1974.

Mining also has traditions going back to the 1600's. The silver mines at Kongsberg were worked until 1957, and the copper mines at Røros until 1977, while the copper mines at Løkken are still in use. But Norway still produces over 100 000 tons of copper concentrate each year, mainly based on pyrites, which also provide valuable sulphur to the chemical industry. This market is now dominated by the sulphur which is produced by the three oil refineries in Norway.

In 1975 Norway produced over 470 000 tons of pyrites, while production of iron ore amounted to over 4 million tons. The two largest extraction sites for pyrites and iron ore are Sydvaranger, which is near the Russian frontier, and Rana, near the Polar Circle. In 1975, 527 000 tons of titanium ore was extracted from Europe's largest deposit, in Sokndal in South-West Norway. About 400 000 tons of coal was produced in Spitzbergen, first and foremost as raw material for a coke works in Rana.

Production of cement approaches 3 million tons a year. Chalkstone is also used as a raw material and auxilliary ingredient in the production of calcium carbide and artificial fertiliser. Quartz is used in the production of ferro-alloys and magnesium, and feldspar and nephelin syenite for ceramics and glass. In addition there is some stone quarried for the building industry, including, granite, marble and slate.

In spite of the fact that the traditional process industry still accounts for about half of Norway's export of industrial goods, the share has been greatly reduced over a period of ten years, — from a level in excess of 70 per cent. This is primarily due to the fact that the machine-shop industry has more than doubled its share, to c. 30 per cent.

The machine-shop industry employed c. 130 000 in 1974. This is the equivalent of $1/3$ of the combined workforce in industry. Shipbuilding, including the building of steel rigs, had a share amounting to 43 000. The gross production value of the machine-shop industry was 25 billion kroner, of which 9 billion kroner was attributable to the shipbuilding industry. Of this total, 3.7 billion kroner was in respect of vessels exceeding 100 gross tons, and with a combined tonnage of 960 000 tons gross.

With regard to export, the shipbuilding industry had an annual increase of 25 per cent on average during the period 1963—73. This is almost 2.5 times the average increase for the industry. The electro-technical industry, with 23 000 employees in 1974, had an almost equally rapid growth — with nearly 23 per cent per year, on average.

Foreign ownership interests are proportionately strongly represented in the electro-technical industry. Firms with a foreign ownership share of more than 20 per cent account for 40 per cent of the employment in this branch. Another characteristic is that 60 per cent of those employed work for companies which, to a significant extent, supply their products to official instances in Norway. This is particularly the case with the electricity supply, telecommunications and defence.

Within the electro-technical industry, the electronic industry has experienced particularly rapid growth, with a doubling of its turnover in a four year period 1970—73. Norway's shipping environment has afforded a specially fertile ground for parts of the electronic industry. This environment has also stimulated the development of other types of advanced shipping equipment, such as hydraulic deck machinery, loading and off-loading systems, steering equipment and others.

The Norwegian machine industry employed 27 000 people in 1974, the same number was employed in another main group within the machine-shop industry — the production of metal goods.

The food and leisure industry is the second largest main group in Norwegian industry. In spite of an increase in exports amounting to 15 per cent a year from 1963—73, this group is naturally directed primarily at the domestic market.

The same is true of the clothing industry, with a good 27 000 employees in 1974, and the furniture and decoration industry with 10 000 employees. As particularly labour-intensive industries, they have been extra badly hit by the cost increases. Import has eroded a lot of the domestic market, and it is difficult to compete on the export market. All the same, some manufacturers — especially in the furniture industry — have managed to increase their exports through specialisation and concentration on high quality and design.

The chemical industry, including rubber and plastic products, employed 28 600 in 1974. In the years to come, Norway will develop a comprehensive petro-chemical industry, based on raw materials from the North Sea. When the authorities granted permission for the laying of pipelines from Ekofisk to other countries, Norway was assured the option of buying up to 550 000 tons of condensate — NGL — per year, shipped from Teesside in Great Britain, to Norway. These deliveries form the basis for the building of the biggest petro-chemical complex in Norway, situated at Rafnes in Bamble, c. 100 km. south-west of Oslo.

Altogether seven factories, with a combined investment sum of c. 5 billion kroner, will commence during the years 1978—80. The factories were built and are owned, first and foremost by Norsk Hydro, Statoil and the Saga Group, a significant industrial group which is, in its turn, owned by 93 large companies representing shipping, banking, industrial and insurance interests. Norsk Hydro, which also has the main emphasis of its fertiliser and PVC production centred on the same area, operates a cracker with an annual capacity of 300 000 tons of ethyl and 70 000 tons of propylene.

In addition there will be production of vinyl chloride, soda lye, chlorine, LD polyethylene, HD polyethylene, polypropylene and vinyl acetate. The polypropylene factory will be the first in the Nordic countries, which are expected to buy up the total production.

A new oil refinery with an annual capacity of c. 4 million tons was started at Mongstad north of Bergen in 1975. Norsk Hydro has a 30 per cent ownership share, while the balance is owned by the State-run companies Statoil and Norsk Olje — NOROL. Esso started a refinery in the Oslo Fjord in 1960, and Shell started one at Stavanger in 1968, with annual capacities of 5.5 and 3 million tons respectively.

AGRICULTURE AND FORESTRY

The cultivated area in Norway totals c. 2 million acres. This is the equivalent of just under 3 per cent of the surface area, excluding Spitzbergen and Jan Mayen. Only half consists of open fields, the remaining 1 million acres comprise meadows and pastures. Almost all farmers own the farms themselves. In 1975 there were c. 140 000 employed in agriculture, compared with c. 160 00 in 1972, when there were 128 000 holdings of at least 1¹/₄ acres. 43 800 farmers, — c. ¹/₃ — had farming as their sole means of support. For 27 500 it was the most important activity, while somewhat in excess of 56 000 had another major form of employment. About 117 000 work years were completed in agriculture, and about 10 000 in forestry.

As recently as in 1959 there were nearly 200 000 holdings of at least 1¹/₄ acres.

In spite of a structural rationalisation, the majority of Norwegian farms are small. In 1975 there were barely 600 farms with an acreage of 125 acres or more. About 25 000 farms had an acreage of at least 25 acres, while about 72 000 had between 5 and 25 acres, and a good 19 000 were between 5 and 1¹/₄ acres.

Forestry means a lot to the farmers in the interior. Many farmers have their own forests, or they take jobs as forestry workers. Along the coast, agriculture is combined with fishing.

The farming season is short, so that the spring work and the harvest requires intensive working efforts. But since incomes from agriculture cannot compete with the levels which obtain in other industries, the farmer and his family must do nearly all the work themselves. Hired help accounts for only 5 per cent of the work effort.

The mechanisation of agriculture has progressed far, however, in spite of somewhat difficult topo-

Farms are highly mechanised. This picture shows a forage harvester at work in Romsdalen, Western Norway.

graphy. From 1949 to 1975 the number of tractors has increased from barely 10 000 to almost 125 000. There were nearly 28 000 threshers and c. 14 500 combine harvesters. In 1969 there were 30 000 potato-picking machines and 50 000 milk machines registered.

Domestic animals play the most important role in Norwegian agriculture, which in 1975 consisted of 900 000 cattle, 670 000 pigs, 1.6 million sheep and 3.8 million poultry. The number of holdings with cows has been reduced from c. 150 000 in 1959 to c. 50 000 in 1975. But with 380 000, the milk production is maintained at 1.8 million tons a year. A further c. 100 000 tons of red meat are produced as well as 75 000 tons of pork, 40 000 tons of eggs and nearly 4 000 tons of wool.

Of the total cultivated area, about 900 000 acres are used as meadows which provide somewhat in excess of 2 million tons of hay. On the average the grazing season for cows lasts for 121 days, and that of sheep for 154 days. Fully cultivated pastures amount to 115 000 acres. In addition to the actual 2 million acres of cultivated land, there are 208 000 acres of natural pasture land.

Altogether, Norway is more than self-sufficient with regard to products from domestic animals, and semi-self-sufficient with regard to grain.

Most of the food grain is imported, while that produced in Norway is mostly used as fodder. But there is a slight increase in the utilisation of Norwegian grain for human consumption. Some 630 000 tons of feed concentrates are imported annually out of a total consumption of 1.4 million tons.

The annual production of fruit amounts to c. 80 000, and for cultivated berries just under 40 000 tons, with vegetables amounting to 130 000 tons. Large quantities of fruit and vegetables are imported at certain times of the year.

Agriculture has its own cooperatives for the purpose of buying and selling, and strong organisations which negotiate with the authorities with regard to prices and subsidies. In recent years agriculture has been granted annual income increments of between 20 and 40 per cent, in order to even out the discrepancy in comparison with other industries. It is important to maintain a certain level of self-sufficiency, and to slow down the rate of exodus from the country districts.

A number of farmers also raise fur-producing animals. The stock has stood at about 1.5 million mink and 300 000 blue fox in recent years. Norway also has a stock of c. 140 000 tame reindeer, but this activity is conducted principally by the Lapps.

Forestry

About ²/₃ of the forest in Norway is owned by farmers, while the rest is owned by the State, the municipalities, limited companies and non-local individuals. Almost 10 million acres of productive forest area is owned by local farmers. The State owns about 1 million acres, plus 0.55 million acres of common land. Local common ground covers rather less than half a million acres of productive forest. In both types of common land, the local population has retained certain rights of utilisation, including cutting of evergreen timber for own use, either as firewood or building materials.

In the 1973—74 season there was slightly more than 9.5 cubic metres of untrimmed timber cut in Norway. Of this amount, 760 000 cub.m. was used on the farms. 8.3 million cub.m. of evergreen timber was sold together with

357 000 cub.m. of deciduous timber. In addition there were c. 100 000 cub.m. of firewood sold, of which nearly $^3/_4$ was deciduous.

From the 1500's and up to the beginning of this century, timber was Norway's most important export commodity. There is still nearly $^1/_2$ a million cub.m. exported a year, and with domestic consumption included, the timber industry consumed c. 3 million cub. m. of timber in 1973. There was a further c. 1 million cub.m. used in connection with wood fibre and hardboard, while wood processing accounted for 6.4 million cub.m. The shortfall was covered by lumber imports, mainly from Sweden and Finland.

The felling of Norwegian timber for sale varies from 6.5 to 8.5 million cub.m. per year, while an annual growth of c. 13 million cub.m. should form the basis for an annual production of 10.5 million cub.m. on the average.

Almost 140 000 people are partly employed in forestry, although the majority have farming as their principal occupation, so that the total number of work years is estimated as being 10 000. Felling has traditionally been a winter occupation, with drawing the timber by horse and floating it down the rivers on the spring floods. Winter is still the main season, but the work has become mechanised, with motor saws, tractors, cable railway and winches.

State grants are given in respect of the building of forest vehicle roads, which had a total length of c. 60 000 km. in 1975. About 2 000 km. is built annually, including tractor and winter roads. As recently as in 1960, nearly 3.5 million cub.m. of timber was floated downstream. In 1974 the total was c. 800 000 cub.m. Lorries and the railway have taken over.

In addition to the c. 10 000 work years in forestry, there is an additional c. 11 000 work years in industries which produce lumber and wooden goods, and c. 21 000 work years in wood processing.

All Norwegian forests are inspected by official instances, who also advise private forest owners with regard to the protection of resources. A tax on timber goes towards the cost of re-forestation. C. 90 000 acres are planted every year, and will be ready for felling in 50—100 years. Systematic efforts have been introduced with regard to drainage and fertilising in order to increase yield.

FISHING AND WHALING

Norwegian fishermen caught a total of 3.1 million tons of fish in 1976, to an initial value of 2.5 billion kroner. Fish species which are mainly used as a raw material for oil and meal — first and foremost capelin — constitute about 75 per cent of the catch and about 40 per cent of the initial value. Between 10 and 12 per cent of the catch is frozsen and there are some 230 freezing plants along the coast. Between 80 and 85 per cent of the catch is exported, and fish meal and frozen fillets have each about a 20 per cent share of the total value. Stockfish, dried fish and salted fish still have the greatest share of the export market — with about 30 per cent altogether. Less than 1 per cent of the catch is consigned to the canning industry, although cans of fish enjoy an export value of nearly 10 per cent of the total.

Stockfish and dried fish have been principal Norwegian export commodities for hundreds of years. In 1976 a total of over 70 000 tons was exported, to a value of 920 million kroner. The export of frozen fish fillets totalled 90 000 tons with a value of 650 million kroner. Most of the fish is ground up into raw materials for oil and meal, which is primarily used as fodder. In 1976 exports of fish

Fishing with nets on the Lofothavet. A large part of the catch is still taken by means of conventional nets, lines and hand-lines. The fleet is dominated by small vessels.

meal totalled 415 000 tons to a value of 730 million kroner.

Norwegian fjords and fishing banks are spawning grounds for large numbers of cod, herring and other northern Atlantic fish species. The coastal and bank fishing continues to be the most important. Vessels which fish further than 200 nautical miles off the coast or along the coasts of other countries, have a share of the total catch amounting to c. 20 per cent. The last 10 years have seen the building of many large vessels with modern equipment. Hydraulic powerblocks manipulate seine nets which are big enough to encompass the largest type of sports stadium, including the terraces. In addition to the modern navigational equipment, the vessels are equipped with electronic fish-finding apparatus.

But a large part of the catch is still taken by normal nets, lines and hand-lines, and small vessels dominate the fishing fleet. Of a total of c. 27 500 motorised fishing boats in 1974, 20 000 were open wooden boats of slightly more than 3 gross tons on average. Of the boats with decks, only about 600 were made of steel.

About 860 fishing boats were over 50 gross tons. Of these, only c. 70 were of 500 tons or more. Thirteen factory trawlers were over 900 tons.

In 1974 Norway had a total of c.

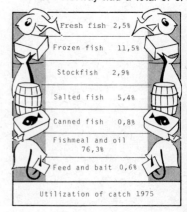

Fresh fish 2,5%
Frozen fish 11,5%
Stockfish 2,9%
Salted fish 5,4%
Canned fish 0,8%
Fishmeal and oil 76,3%
Feed and bait 0,6%

Utilization of catch 1975

36 500 fishermen, as opposed to a total of 61 000 in 1960 and 86 000 in 1948. Just over half have fishing as their sole occupation, and including those who have fishing as their principal occupation, the total comes up to 26 500. The rest have fishing as a secondary occupation. Along the coast fishing is combined with farming. Many farmers and fishermen also take secondary employment in the building industry.

Most fishing vessels are owned by one or a few people, and the crews are paid by shares in the catch. Fishermen have strong organisations, with Norges Fiskarlag (Norwegian Fishermen's Association) as the main organisation, and 13 sales organisations which regulate prices for the different fish species and geographical areas. The object is to ensure good and reasonably stable prices.

Over-fishing of certain species has increased the importance of international controls. Norway has entered into a number of bilateral agreements. In 1975 Norway created a number of coastal zones where trawling was forbidden, and Norway has taken a lead in connection with UN cooperation regarding the extension of fishing zones and the establishment of economic zones 200 nautical miles from the coast.

Special negotiations have been conducted with the Soviet Union regarding the border in the Barents Sea, which is involved in the movement pattern of fish stocks which are of special importance for Norway. The fish, of course, move around untrammelled by the zone boundaries, so that the catch quotas have to apply in total terms. Many people regard the market problems as being the worst, following the introduction of a certain degree of protection for fish stocks.

The Norwegian fish exports are primarily directed at the EEC

Norway exports large amounts of frozen fish fillets.

which takes a 40 per cent share. The EFTA countries are falling off with less than 20 per cent, while the USA takes 10—12 per cent.

Whaling — Seal Hunting

After the Norwegian, Svend Foyn, invented the harpoon gun in the 1860's, whaling became an important industry. Norway was the leading nation in the world in the 1930's with regard to pelagic whaling, with almost 400 000 tons of whale-oil production out of a record catch of c. 600 000 tons in the record year of 1931.

Norway was one of the principal whaling nations after the war, and efforts were made to introduce quota regulations in order to protect the whale stocks. When such agreement was not forthcoming, Norway speedily ran down her whaling activities at the beginning of the 1960's.

Norway is now only engaged in catching small whales in northern waters, and the whale meat is sold for human consumption. In 1976 the initial value of the catch was c. 30 million kroner.

Seal hunting off Newfoundland is the scene of diminishing Norwegian participation. In 1974, 30 vessels returned with 114 000 seals with an initial value of almost 20 million kroner. In 1976 the corresponding figures were: 26, 85 000 and 12 million.

SERVICE-PRODUCING ACTIVITIES

The service-producing activities have experienced the greatest degree of growth in Norway in recent years in terms of employment, and involve c. 54 per cent of the total employed (1976), as opposed to 65 per cent in the USA. During the period 1960—1970, employment in service-producing activities increased by 150 000, while industry increased by 50 000 while the primary trades lost 95 000. The net growth of the combined numbers employed was 110 000. In 1970—1980 both the primary trades and industry are expected to fall off, by as much as 50 000 together, while the service activities are expected to grow almost as quickly as before.

In 1976 there were 866 000 work years completed in service-producing activities. Official, social and private service-production accounted for 432 000 work years, almost 50 000 more than 5 years previously. In the retail trade there was an increase in the same period of 7 000 work years, bringing the total to 213 000. The third large group was communications, excluding shipping, with 114 000 work years.

Commercial service-production accounted for 37 000 work years, bank and insurance for 34 000 and hotel and restaurant operation for 32 000.

While industry, mining and power production accounted for c. 42 billion kroner — or about $\frac{1}{4}$ the Gross National Product of 170 billion kroner — official, social and private service-producing activities had a share amounting to 32.4 billion, retail trade a share of 33 billion, and communications (excluding shipping) a share of almost 11 billion.

In the transport sector, excluding the railways and foreign travel, there were almost 19 000 firms in Norway in 1974, employing nearly 56 000. Ancillary services involved nearly 1 000 companies with 9 500 employees.

The three large State services within communications — the railways, postal service and telecommunications — each had c. 18 000 employees.

Service-producing activities such as e.g. banking, insurance, retail trade etc. involved nearly 140 000 employees in 1974. In education and the health and social sectors there were 250 000 employees. Official administration, defence, police and the judicial system had a combined total of 85 000 employees. There were 130 000 employed by the State, and 120 000 employed in local government.

SHIPPING

Norway has the fourth largest merchant fleet in the world, following Liberia, Japan and Great Britain. With 2 833 ships totalling 27.6 million gross tons at the beginning of 1977, Norway had 7 per cent of the world tonnage, as opposed to 10 in 1967. Until 1974 shipping accounted for about $\frac{1}{3}$ of Norway's total currency income. The protracted crisis in shipping which was occasioned by the oil crisis of 1973 has reduced that share to $\frac{1}{4}$, and Norway's oil export will provide substantial surpluses in the years to come. But shipping will continue to play an important role in Norway's commercial life. Norway's c. 200 shipping companies are also strongly involved in the oil industry, both with regard to drilling platforms and supply vessels, and through participation in new oil companies, first and foremost the Saga Group.

The tanker fleet, with 353 vessels totalling 15.5 million gross tons, the equivalent of c. 9 per cent of the world tanker tonnage, had about 100 vessels laid up in 1976, amounting to nearly $^1/_3$ of the country's total tonnage. But· expressed as a proportion of the ships in overseas traffic, the share amounted to barely 10 per cent. There has therefore been little unemployment among the crew workforce, which in 1975 totalled 28 400. Almost 20 per cent of these were foreigners.

Traditionally $^2/_3$ of the tanker fleet has sailed on long-term contracts. Such contracts involved $^1/_3$ of the fleet as recently as the beginning of 1977. Individual tanker companies have enjoyed large profits even during the crisis years. Others, which have concentrated on normal traffic and drilling rigs have experienced considerable liquidity problems. A number of these companies were, however, saved by means of a pioneering Norwegian venture: A State Guarantee Institute for Ships and Drilling Rigs with voluntary participation by shipping companies and creditors. There is no official subsidising, just a State guarantee of up to 4 billion kroner. By means of agreements between the shipping companies, shipbuilders and finance institutions, the Institute attempts to prevent lack of liquidity on the part of the shipping companies, as a result of the oil crisis, forcing the sale of ships or drilling rigs abroad for prices which are lower than those which are acceptable in terms of social economics.

A particular feature of Norwegian shipping is the low age of the vessels. As much as 85 per cent of the fleet is less than 10 years old, and the average age is 6 years. In addition, Norwegian shipowners have concentrated on advanced special-purpose vessels, often in cooperation with Norwegian yards and Norwegian manufacturers of shipping equipment.

Furthermore, Oslo has become one of the leading world centres of shipbroking; the Norwegian classification company is one of the world's largest, the finance institutions have the best maritime expertise; and great attention is paid to education and research.

Shipping satisfies the social need of a capital- and know-how-characterised trading activity with high profitability, and recruitment is primarily from districts with weak commercial activities.

Norwegian shipping is owned and operated by private persons. While other countries are mainly dominated by a few large shipping companies, Norway has c. 200 which are involved in overseas traffic. Over 90 per cent of the tonnage never docks at Norwegian ports. Norway is a strong supporter of free international competition, and against all kinds of preferences and subsidies.

Since the autumn of 1974 Norwegian shipowners have cancelled orders for c. 12 million tons deadweight. Nonetheless, Norway's overseas fleet increased by 7 million t.dw. in 1976 to 39 million t.dw. At the beginning of 1977 there was still 9 million t.dw. laid up. But the number of vessels laid up was reduced to 65 out of a total of 1 173 vessels engaged in overseas traffic.

Norway was among the first to concentrate upon supertankers, and has since pioneered the development of gas and chemical tankers, and combination vessels. In 1975 Norway had 45 gas tankers which was the equivalent of 10

The Norwegian overseas fleet's composition — new year 1976.

Type of vessel	Total	Gross tons	% of total gross tonnage
Cruise ships	14	245 000	1
Ferries	15	54 500	0.2
Gas tankers	45	370 000	1.5
Other tankers	278	13 650 000	54.1
Oretankers	19	1 745 000	6.9
Bulktankers	37	2 030 000	8
Ore carriers	12	240 000	1
Carbulk carriers	42	710 000	2.8
Other bulk carriers	161	4 305 000	17.1
Refrigerator/freezer ships	24	80 000	0.3
Ro-ro, LASH, etc.	74	690 000	2.7
Other dry cargo vessels	345	1 050 000	4.2
Supply ships	94	55 000	0.2
	1 160	25 225 000	100.0

per cent of the world tonnage of this type of vessel. In the case of chemical tankers the respective figures were 28 and 30 per cent, and for combination vessels, 57 and 16 per cent.

FOREIGN TRADE

As most of the small countries with a high standard of living, Norway has to concentrate on specialised production and a very extrovert economy. The export of goods and services — especially shipping services — constitute c. 40 per cent of the gross national product altogether, and imports account for c. 50 per cent. Only about 20 per cent of the imports are for consumption. Investment takes 30 per cent, and the balance of 50 per cent consists of raw materials and other materials for processing.

Fish and forestry products, ores and metals have long been important Norwegian export goods. The value of cheap hydro-electric power has been exported 'contained' in electro-metallurgic products, especially aluminium — which is based on the import of aluminium oxide — and ferroalloys, based on Norwegian quartz.

The export of finished goods has increased rapidly following the lowering of tariff barriers, as have also the import of such goods. Sweden has long been our principal partner in this trade, and if petroleum is excluded, Sweden remains the country's most important trading partner.

In 1976 the value of Norway's goods exports rose by 18 per cent, and goods imports by 19 per cent, excluding shipping. Trade with Sweden comprised 16 per cent of exports, and 17 per cent of imports.

Great Britain took 15 per cent of Norway's goods exports, when oil is excluded. Including oil, the share increases to 32 per cent. Rather more than 10 per cent of the oil which is transported through a pipeline from the Ekofisk field to Teesside in Great Britain, is returned to Norway by ship. Including the oil the British share of Norway's goods imports is c. 15 per cent, with cars and machinery as the other main items.

West Germany has 20 per cent of Norway's goods imports. Here

Trade 1976

Most important partners	Exports excluding ships Billions of kr.	Increase % from 1975	Imports excluding ships Billions of kr.	Increase % from 1975
Sweden	6	3%	9	9%
Denmark	2.5	4,7%	3.3	17%
Finland	0.9	6%	1.4	26%
United Kingdom	12.2	44%	5.6	14%
Of which crude oil ..	6.5	200%	0.6	380%
West Germany	4	14,5%	7.6	15%
Netherlands	1.4	21%	2.9	70%
France	1	÷ 12%	2.2	25%
Italy	0.7	27%	1	23%
Belgium, Lux.	0.6	÷ 7%	1.5	14%
USSR	0.4	÷ 13%	0.4	6,4%
USA	2	1,7%	3.9	7,5%
Japan	0.4	35%	1.8	45%

too, cars and machinery are predominant. At present West Germany is Norway's 3rd largest export market, with a share of c. 10.5 per cent. This will increase with the deliveries of gas from Ekofisk to Emden in West Germany.

Altogether the EC took nearly 60 per cent of Norway's goods eports, while the EC share of import amounted to 46 per cent. Western Europe as a whole took 82 per cent of Norway's exports and accounted for 70 per cent of imports.

The USA, which takes a good 5 per cent of Norway's exports — especially aluminium, frozen fish and furs, accounts for 10 per cent of the imports — primarily machinery and bread grain.

Japan, which has also assorted itself in Norway with, among other things, cars and electronics, has moreover a 30 per cent share of the import of new ships to Norway. Sweden and West Germany supply c. 20 and 25 per cent respectively of the new ships which are imported.

During most of the post-war years, Norway has had a trading deficit. This has been covered by means of private and official loans for investments. Shipping has mostly been financed abroad, thanks to the high credit rating of the shipping companies. After the petroleum discoveries, Norway as a whole has been able to take up virtually unlimited loans.

In a few years Norway will be a large exporter of capital. This will partly take place through the purchase of bonds and stocks, but also through the establisment of Norwegian industries in other countries.

Norwegian exports of know-how and of complete projects have increased considerably in recent years. This partly takes place in the form of joint-venture with interests in the host country, and partly by the establishment of wholly Norwegian subsidiary companies. Norway will probably follow the example of Sweden with expansion throughout the world.

In addition, Sweden is very interested in establishing closer cooperation with Norway, with agreements in respect of deliveries of energy to Sweden, and the transfer of technology in the opposite direction. West Germany too has begun negotitations with Norway with similar aims.

Balance of trade 1976

Exports: **Billion kr**		Imports: **Billion kr**	
Goods	38.7	Goods	56.1
Ships, new	2.3	Ships	7.8
Ships, older	2.7	Shipping expenses	8.4
Gross freights	16.8	Passenger traffic	3.4
Passenger traffic	2.2	Other services	9.4
Other services	6.5		85.1
	69.2		

Communications

Scattered settlements, the country's great north-south length with deep valleys, high mountains and great fiords, as well as the climatic conditions, are factors which greatly add to the difficulties and cost of constructing and maintaining a nationwide transportation system as well as telecommunications in Norway.

International Communications

All-year scheduled sailings by modern passenger ships connect Norwegian ports to major cities in several countries. Railroad connections with the Continent run via Sweden and Denmark. The roads are linked with those of the other countries on the Scandinavian Peninsula, and large car ferries maintain regular connections with Denmark, Germany and the United Kingdom. There are regular international flights to major cities abroad.

ROADS AND ROAD TRAFFIC

The Norwegian road network is very extensive. There are a total of 78 116 kilometres of public roads, of which 24 977 kilometres are state road, 30 856 kilometres country roads and 22 283 kilometres municipal roads. In addition there is also a well developed network of private forest roads for the transportation of timber.

A total of 36 976 kilometres (47%) of the public roads are hardsurfaced, mostly bituminous paving. The remainder is gravel-surfaced. A comprehensive construction and reconstruction programme for the road system has been followed for the past decade, and has resulted in a good network for road transportation. Major efforts are now being made to achieve balanced transportation systems in the urban areas in order to establish and maintain good environmental qualities.

The motor vehicle population has increased rapidly during the past decade. At the end of 1976 a total of 1 170 842 motor vehicles were registered in Norway. Of these 1 022 918 were private cars. This is equivalent to 3.9 inhabitants per private car. It is estimated that the density will increase annually by approx. 0.2 inhabitants per car. In addition to the motor vehicles

The communications network in Norway is joined together by thousands of bridges. This is Kvalsund Bridge in Finnmark.

come 448 854 motor cycles, agricultural tractors, trailers, etc.

Buses employed in public passenger transportation totalled 7276 at the end of 1974. The transportation work during 1974 amounted to 4.058 million passenger kilometres. Bus operation is generally unprofitable, but nevertheless essential to communities lacking other transport facilities. Subsidies to bus operation reached a record high of approx. 320 million kr. in 1976.

RAILWAYS

Norway has 4257 kilometres of railways, of which 16 kilometres are owned by private companies and the balance by the Norwegian State Railways. The railways are mainly single tracked and of normal gauge. Electrification has been introduced on 58 per cent of the tracks. Steam has been completely supplamented by electric and diesel engines since 1970.

The main railways radiate out from Oslo. Southwards and eastwards to Sweden, northwards to Trondheim and Bodø, northwestwards to Åndalsnes and Fagernes, westwards to Bergen and southwestwards to Kristiansand and Stavanger. In Northern Norway there is a railway used for iron ore transportation from Kiruna in Sweden to Narvik.

During 1976 the railways carried 32.7 million passengers an average distance of 61 kilometres. Transport of freight amounted to 28.8 million tons, resulting in transportation work of 2709 million ton kilometres. The railways were operated at a total deficit of 579.9 million kroner during 1976.

COASTAL TRANSPORTATION

Extensions of the road systems with bridges and new ferry connections across the fiords, have gradually reduced the demand for passenger and freight lines along

53

The railway also has its problems on the mountain routes in the winter. Here we see a rotating snowplough in action on the Bergen line.

the coast. But although the demand has been reduced, coastal shipping services are of major importance for the communities along the coast.

Approximately 440 vessels with a gross tonnage exceeding 100 000 tons are employed in regular coastal services. Some 250 vessels, sailing as ferries between public roads, carried 38 million passengers and 12 million motor vehicles during 1976.

In addition approximately 1000 vessels are engaged in coastal tramp trade. It is estimated that nearly 60 per cent of the national goods transportation work was carried out by coastal shipping during 1974.

AVIATION

DNL (Det Norske Luftfartsselskap), was founded by shipping interests in 1927. In order to open a route to New York, a venture considered too costly for DNL alone, the Scandinavian Airlines System was formed in 1946 in cooperation with the national airlines of Denmark and Sweden. In 1948 the three companies also pooled their European traffic, and in 1950 they merged all their resources and activities in a new SAS organization. Simultaneously the governments of the three countries assumed 50 per cent of the capital of the respective airlines, which then became parent companies of SAS. Norway and Denmark hold 2/7 of the total capital invested in SAS, while Sweden holds 3/7.

Domestically, a private airline, Braathens SAFE Air Transport, has nearly the same amount of traffic as SAS. Another private airline, Widerøes Flyveselskap A/S, provides commuter service to 30 communities along the Norwegian coast.

SAS maintains regular non-stop flights from Norway to New York and Seattle. Other intercontinental SAS flights originate in Copenhagen, which is served from Oslo 13 times daily. European destinations are either served by direct flights or via Copenhagen.

In 1976 SAS carried 7.1 million passengers. As of 1974 it was third largest on European carrier routes, and the eighth largest on the North American routes.

There are twenty airfields in Norway receiving trunk line air traffic and charter traffic. For local scheduled aviation there are another 19 STOL (short take-off and landing) airfields, as well as two heliports on the islands Röst and Værøy.

The establishing of feeder line air service from STOL-airfields to the national trunk airline has improved transport possibilities for the population living in the outer districts, particularly in the northern part of the country.

POSTAL SERVICE

The postal service was established in 1647 and is operated as a government directorate. The first postage stamp was issued in 1855. Norway has 3062 post offices (Dec. 1975) which annually handle 1 085 million mail items, including 664 million letterpost. The Post Office (Postverket) also operates a giro service and a postal savings bank.

TELECOMMUNICATION

At the end of 1975 there were 1,41 million telephones in Norway (35 per 100 inhabitants). Approximately 90 per cent of the telephones are automatically operated. The number of subscribers connected with the national and international long distance direct dialling system is rapidly being increased. The telephone and telex services are operated by the state telegraph service (Televerket).

Environmental Protection

In Norway, work in connection with questions of environmental protection is conducted by, and coordinated through, a separate Ministry of the Environment, which was created in 1972. The sphere of operations of the Ministry of the Environment has been steadily enlarged so that it today covers, inter alia, area-planning, administration and protection of the natural resources, measures directed against pollution and noise, securing of open-air areas and protection of cultural environments.

Protection of Natural Resources

Norwegians are in the fortunate position of having access to large

and varied natural areas. Norwegian nature includes, among other things, skerries, inland lakes, and great forest and mountain areas. But the needs of industrial expansion and housing for new areas often come into conflict with the desire to maintain the natural areas in their present state. One of the principal objectives of Norwegian environmental policy is to preserve a number of areas as far as possible unspoiled so that the variegated animal life and flora may be protected, and so that we are able to satisfy the steadily increasing requirement for natural areas for recreation and open-air activities. Since 1962 there have been 13 national parks created throughout the country with a combined area amounting to 5 043 square kilometres. In addition to these there have been almost 150 smaller nature reserves and landscape protection areas established. Large areas are also controlled for open-air purposes. A number of large and small waterways are permanently or temporarily protected against hydro-electric power development. These waterways constitute altogether about 10% of the country's exploitable hydro-electric resources.

Work against Pollution

Even though Norway is situated far to the North and on the periphery of industrialised Europe, the country is strongly affected by pollution sources outside its own national frontiers. Wind and ocean currents carry pollution with them across large distances. The large quantities of SO_2-gas which are released from Central Europe and the British Isles represent a great problem for Norway. These, and other forms of air-borne pollution are carried across to Norway by the wind, after which it is mingled with the precipitation which falls over the southern parts of the country. Such pollution rend the forest floor and the waterways acidic, with resultant damage to vegetation and fish deaths. The Norwegian Government is specifically interested in concluding international agreements aimed at the reduction of polluted effluence, and is actively working towards that end.

The international character of pollution problems has necessitated comprehensive international cooperation in other areas as well. The Oslo Convention, the Paris Convention and the International Convention of 1973 in respect of pollution from shipping have laid the foundation for a steadily more

Blow-out on the Bravo platform, spring 1977. The oil industry has presented the Norwegian environmental protection authorities with new and exacting problems.

comprehensive international co-operation with regard to questions of ocean pollution.

The Ministry of the Environment is doing as much as possible towards the limitation of pollution problems within Norway's own boundaries. One of the most salient principles behind Norwegian environmental protection policy is that those who occasion pollution must accept the legal and economic responsibility for the damage which such pollution causes, and the prevention of such pollution problems reoccurring in the future. In accordance with this policy, those responsible for the managment of industry, agriculture, forestry and fishing are required to carry out a number of measures which are designed to limit the extent of pollution and noise problems. In order to ensure that these measures are carried out, the State has established a number of supportive and loan arrangements for the purchase of the necessary environmental protection equipment. The municipal authorities are responsible for the establishment of waste disposal systems and the building of cleansing plants in order to prevent pollution from housing areas.

The oil industry on the Norwegian continental shelf has presented the Norwegian environment protection authorities with new, demanding tasks. The Ministry of the Environment has faced the companies which are engaged in oil activities on the Norwegian part of the continental shelf with the most stringent requirements. The companies have been required to provide mechanical oil prevention equipment which is capable of dealing with up to 8 000 tons of oil per day in the event of an uncontrolled blow-out on the continental shelf. In the opinion of the Norwegian authorities, the equipment which is available on the market today does not afford suf-

The site of the Denofa-Lilleborg A/S plant in Fredrikstad.

ficient protection against large-scale oilspills. The Storting has therefore made 10 million kroner available for the development of improved oil prevention equipment. Several projects are under way which are aimed at the development of systems and equipment which can collect oil-spill on the open sea.

At the same time the State-administered oil prevention preparedness is being built up at full speed. This is necessary in order to deal with oil-spills from shipping, and is designed first and foremost as a coastal preparedness. The Storting has made 55 million kroner available for the purchase of equipment and the organisation of the State administered oil prevention preparedness. The equipment, which consists of booms, suction units and oil prevention vessels, will be housed in 12 depots along the coast and will be in position by the Spring of 1978.

Labour relations and protection

Trade Union democracy among Norwegian workers, with 70% of the total workforce belonging to a suitable union, is one of the best developed democracies of its type in the world.

The wage agreement system was established as early as the 1870's. The Norwegian Federation of Trade Unions (Landsorganisasjonen — LO) was founded in 1899 and the Norwegian Employers' Confederation (Norsk Arbeidsgiverforening — NAF) was founded in 1900. There has never been any proscription of the right to form trade unions in Norway.

The main agreement which was negotiated in 1935 between the LO and the NAF, represents the Constitution of the economic life — it includes rules pertaining to the freedom to organise trade unions, the duty to maintain industrial peace during the course of a wage agreement, the right of negotiation, the correct procedure in the case of an official strike, the conditions and the amount of notice to be given in connection with lay-offs, etc. The main agreement is revised every other year.

Individual fundamental agreements have been drawn up in respect of special groups of workers like local government employees, co-operative employees, workers in the Labour Press, in the building and construction industry, etc.

The right to strike, to impose boycotts, and the employers' right of lockout have always been legal weapons in principle in the economic life of Norway, when the struggle has been concerned with the establishment of a wage agreement, and what the content of such an agreement is to be.

Legally imposed arbitration has been made use of at certain times with regard to wage-talk breakdowns. Arbitration is involved today if both parties wish for a decision by an independent authority, or if the Storting decides that the wage impasse is to be resolved by legal means because it is a source of threat to life or health or the fundamental economic or social interests of the society (key industries).

In 1976 there were altogether 8 lawful and 20 unlawful strikes registered in Norway.

The definitive interpretation of the principal points of a wage agreement is determined by the Labour Court. This is a court with representatives from all walks of economic life as well as from the State. The day-to-day wage wrangles — several thousands in total every year — are resolved by the parties involved, independently.

Legal wrangles which concern the interpretation of the individual employee's agreement with the company, or the interpretation of a statuary enactment which controls the employee's legal position, will be resolved by special local Labour Courts from 1977. This is a new departure in the history of Norwegian labour tribunals, and the courts are composed of representatives from both the employee and employer sides, besides the legally-trained judges.

The principal agreement between the Federation of Norwegian Trade Unions and the Norwegian Employers' Confederation provides for the setting up of company committees from 1966 in companies with more than 100 employees, and departmental committees where there are more than 200 employees. These cooperative instances are to afford advise which is aimed at promoting production at the same time as increasing the congeniality of the jobs. The committees are not granted authority to make decisions.

Worker representation in instances in companies which do have the authority to make decisions (the Board, corporate assembly, etc.) is covered in the 1972 amendments to the Joint Stock Companies Act. Such representation is extended through new legislation and wage agreements, with the object of introducing company democracy in all private and public industries and branches of commerce in Norway. This right of participation in decision-making with regard to the employees, is currently based on the principal of $2/3$ of the members of such organs representing the owners of the company, with the other $1/3$ representing the employees.

WORKER PROTECTION

Protection of the working environment and the legal protection for the individual employee is partly determined by Law and partly by agreements. The State Labour Inspection ensures, on behalf of the Government, that the laws and regulations which apply to worker protection and the working environment, are respected. The working week is restricted to 40 hours for day workers. Working time shall not exceed 9 hours per day. Overtime for the individual worker must not exceed 200 hours per annum.

Companies which employ in excess of 50 persons are required to establish a working environment committee which is to consist of an equal number of members representing the workers and the company. Safety and health personnel are to be represented on the committee, but without voting rights. As chairman of the committee, alternate representatives of the employees and the company are to serve. The committee is empowered to require the employer to implement concrete protective measures which are covered by the provisions of the Act. If the measure is not implemented within the stipulated time limit, the State Labour Inspection makes a final decision on the matter.

In the companies there will be one or more safety delegates chosen who will safeguard the interests of the workers in matters pertaining to the working environment. The safety delegate has the authority to take decisions with regard to questions which involve work being halted which he considers as constituting a danger to health or life. If such a decision to halt an operation is taken by a safety delegate, he will not be liable for any kind of compensation in respect of economic loss which may be occasioned by such a stoppage.

In order to protect the employee against the abuse of personal data which is registered by the company via computer-based systems or other means, a framework agreement has been agreed between the main organisations involved in industry and commerce, etc. with regard to the collection, use, etc. of personal data, besides laws which cover both private and public registers of personal data.

Measures which concern worker protection and the working environment, are designed to prevent industrial accidents and occupational deseases. In spite of continually improved measures against industrial injuries, there are over c. 25 000 serious industrial accidents at Norwegian places of work registered every year. Of these about c. 200 are fatal accidents. Less extensive injuries (involving sick-leave of less than 11 days) amounts to c. 80 000 per year.

The National Insurance includes a special occupational injury benefit, rehabilitation benefit and disability pension arrangement, as well as dependents pensions which ensure a certain economic basis for wholly or partially disabled employees of for surviving partners and children in the event of death. If the industrial injury is ascribable to negligence on the part of the company, the injured person will be eligible for compensation in addition to the benefits granted under National Insurance.

If an employee loses his job because the company is declared bankrupt, he is assured his wages during the period of notice. If unemployment occurs as a result of reductions in the workforce, the closure of the company, etc. the employee will be assured unemployment benefit, day money, grants in respect of travel and removal expenses when moving to a new place of work, grants for training and re-training, etc.

Legislation has established an annual holiday entitlement of four weeks for all workers in Norway, and five weeks for workers over 60 years. The Federation of Norwegian Trade Unions and the Norwegian Employers' Confederation have entered into special wage agreements which supplement the provisions of the National Insurance laws and other legislation. The sick pay arrangement guarantees, for example, the trade union organised employee a supplement to his sick benefit which affords him 90% of his net wage for at least as long as the sick benefit is payable.

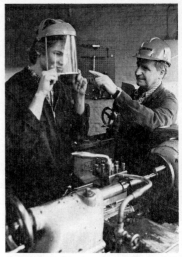

A safety delegate at work in the factory.

The cooperation between the main organisations in commerce and industry and the central authorities has undergone considerable development during recent years. There is some dissension concerning whether or not the general tariff revision which takes place every other year, should be negotiated with each of the unions individually — there are c. 40 of these in the federation — or whether the negotiations should be coordinated through the offices of the federation and be prepared and carried out through direct cooperation with the government. The Norwegian Federation of Trade Unions considers the form of negotiation to be adopted before each tariff revision, i.e. either via individual negotiations with the separate unions, or by means of the so-called «collective agreement» where the State influences the contents of the agreement by the means at its disposal, with immediate reference to the implementation of the tariff revision.

Social Conditions

Norway is often called a welfare state. This refers first and foremost to the fact that we live in a highly industrialised society with a democratic form of government. The welfare state of Norway has a number of characteristics, among which the basic principles are equality of status, the right to work, housing and education, the care of the weak, and social and health security for all. This welfare society has no long history behind it. From the Poor Relief and help for dependents of old times, the last few decades have witnessed a new view of society's duties towards the individual. Private charity and assistance has gradually been replaced by the individual's legal rights through legislation. In Norway since the war, we have enjoyed almost full employment, and our total production during that time has increased by an average of 5 per cent a year. Between the different parts of the country and the various social groupings, an evening out of incomes has taken place, even though there are still considerable discrepancies.

Administration

The main part of the social laws are administered by the Ministry of Social Affairs, but legislation affords central administrative organs outside the Ministry — e.g. The National Social Security Service, The State Temperance Directorate, The National Insurance Court, etc. greater or lesser authority to make decisions on its behalf. The Directorate of Public Health, which is a section of the Ministry of Social Affairs, is responsible for the comprehensive health legislation. It controls and inspects hospitals, the dispensing chemists' service, the supply of pharmaceutical goods, etc. The Chief Administrative Officers of the counties, and the County Medical Officers, and others, carry out various duties within the health and social sectors at the county level.

Municipal autonomy has a strong position from bygone days in Norway within the social sphere, and there are still municipal instances to be found which, according to the statutes, are responsible for the carrying out of important tasks. The reason is that the local government employees and the elected representatives have a better perspective in respect of needs and resources than the central authorities, and are better able to follow up the carrying out of social measures and stimulate local initiative.

THE NATIONAL INSURANCE SCHEME

The insurance system, **The National Insurance Scheme,** has contributed more towards a level of economic security which was hitherto unknown to large groups of the population, than any other social political reform in post-war Norway. From May 1, 1977, the basic amount of the national insurance scheme is 13 400 kroner. The basic pension for single people is the same as this basic figure, while the pension for a married couple who are both entitled to a pension, is 150 per cent of the basic figure. The national insurance scheme is compulsory for all who live in Norway. It was introduced in 1971 when all the individual insurances were combined. It has a wideranging benefit programme and affords aid — besides in respect of age — in cases of illness, physical disability, pregnancy and birth, unemployment, invalidity, death and loss of economic provider. The insurance scheme also affords support to unmarried mothers and divorced and separated people who have children to support. It thus lends good security to the individual in practically all conditions imposed by life. The children's allowance, which is wholly financed by the State, is kept separately from the national insurance scheme, and the same is also true of war pensions and those for certain special occupational groups.

Most of the pensions which come under national insurance scheme consist of two elements: a **basic pension** which is independent of income, and a **supplementary pension** which varies in accordance with the individual's previous income and total number of years in active employment. All benefits under the national insurance scheme are fixed in relation to a **basic figure.** This is adjusted in relation to alterations in the cost of living and the general level of incomes. The national insurance scheme has observed full equality between widows and widowers, as well as with regard to the right to dependency allowances for dependent partners.

National insurance is built on the premise that the best form of aid is help towards self-help. The aim is thus — by means of active rehabilitation measures — to re-establish the individual's ability to work, as far as this is possible. The self-help principle is related to the important tendency which is typical of a productivity society. Social progress and economic development must go hand in hand. Re-training of functionally deficient people and leading them back to a working situation is a sound investment, both from the individual's point of view as well as that of Society. The same attitudes also make themselves felt within the spheres of worker protection and employment. Protective and welfare measures in factories are today not only regarded as being necessary from a humanitarian point of view, but also as measures which contribute to promoting production.

National insurance covers a large spectrum of a society which is constantly changing, and which therefore constantly adjusts itself to changing conditions. One question, among the many which are raised today, is whether too much money is used in connection with the general aid measures, and too little for those in connection with groups which are particularly badly situated. The great increase in the national insurance outlay equally requires reconsideration.

An area where national insurance has had by no means least decisive influence is that of health, in that it not only ensures economic independence in crisis situations, when a person is unable to fend for himself by means of his own work, but asserts itself in terms of payment in connection with illness or birth, both within institutions and without. It is also gradually covering many types of preventive health work, and thus intervenes decisively with regards to the building up of a state of health in the population.

HEALTH

Hardly any country in the world has a more strongly decentralised health service than Norway. The Health Act of 1860 requires there to be a health council in every municipality. The health council

The Norwegian National Insurance Scheme

Pensions and transitional benefits by type of benefit 1976

Benefit	In December 1976		Costs 1976[2]
	Number of recipients	Yearly amount per recipient[1]	
		Kroner	Million kroner
Old age pension	475,075	16,913	6,973,7
Disability pension	146,441	21,159	3,147,9
Survivor's pension/transitionnal benefits (surviving spouse, unmarried person forced to live at home)	45,360	17,755	764,0
Children's pension	24,591	4,780	115,7
Transitional benefits to unmarried mothers	12,482	14,915	176,7
Total	703,949	17,398	11,178,0

[1] Including special supplement and compensation supplement.

[2] Including special supplement, compensation supplement, basic grant and assistance benefit for disabled, assistance benefit for surviving spouse and unmarried mother.

should have its attention directed at all questions pertaining to health in the municipality. The health council's spokesman is the Local Medical officer. The majority of Medical officers are simultaneously private practitioners and members of a number of municipal committees which are concerned with questions of health.

A victorious battle has been waged against serious widespread illnesses such as tuberculosis, poliomyelitis, diphtheria, measles etc. during the first half of the twentieth century. Regular tuberculosis inspections are carried out among the population, and particularly vulnerable groups are kept under special examination. Virtually all small children in Norway are subject to health examinations and undergo a comprehensive vaccination programme. Parents' training in infant care contributes towards the maintenance of a low mortality rate. All men of military service age are subject to a doctor's examination both before and during military service. Many who are employed in industry, and certain other occupational groups, are offered regular health controls by means of company doctor arrangements. The work of the school doctors, school dentists, school psychologists and school nurses forms an important part of the preventive health work for schoolchildren. A network of family counselling offices covers the whole country, and a team of medically trained personnel are able to give help, advice and treatment in connection with matrimonial problems. Other important parts of the preventive health work takes the form of inspection and control of foodstuffs and medicines as well as our 'chemical environment'. By means of internationally approved methods, steps are taken to protect the country from exterior dangerous infections.

Health Institutions

With regard to the development of health institutions, this has taken place for the most part on the initiative of municipal or county council authorities or voluntary organisations. This has frequently led to the size, positioning and function of the health institutions not being assessed beyond the narrow confines of a local context. The economic conditions within the municipality have played an important role. This situation was considerably altered as a result of a Hospital Act in 1970 which made it obligatory for all county councils to build and administer health institutions. The authorities' plans for the development of hospitals directed towards a strong 'front line' of health work which is able to afford the patients assistance as close to their home as possible, and prevent unnecessary admissions to institutions.

Mental Health Protection

The counties are also responsible for the development of institutions within the mental health protection service. Considerable changes have taken place during the course of a couple of generations with regard to the care of the mentally ill. More active forms of treatment have improved conditions for patients and altered people's attitudes towards mental illness. Great emphasis is placed today on the policlinical treatment of patients, and admissions to psychiatric hospitals and clinics are of altogether shorter duration. Most of the patients covered by mental health protection are themselves the ones to seek help with their problems. All institutions where severely mentally ill persons are undergoing treatment or care are subject to an officially appointed control commission.

The health protection for the mentally underdeveloped — the Care for the Mentally Retarded— is organised in Norway on a nationwide basis in accordance with a Storting resolution. The main points of the plan involve the division of the country into self-sufficient areas with institutions for care, protection and training. The development of this care for the mentally retarded will gradually be concentrated more and more on day institutions and other local aid measures.

Physically Handicapped

The physically handicapped constitute a diverse group of people with different needs. As far as the physically handicapped are concerned, the overriding objective of the National Insurance Scheme is that they should first of all be helped to overcome their problems so that they are able to participate in the normal life of the society as far as this is possible. For this reason the rehabilitation and re-socialisation programme is tailor-made for the individual handicapped person's condition. Rehabilitation institutions have been created in all the provinces, affording treatment and rehabilitation which is directed towards the normalisation of the handicapped patients' condition as much as possible. Personnel who are specifically trained for the task, help the physically handicapped to gain suitable employment — on the open market, in protected concerns or in special concerns which are designed for those with a restricted choice of employment. Unlike certain other countries, Norway does not require concerns to employ a certain quota of physically handicapped people. Such an arrangement is not wanted by the handicapped themselves.

A lot is being done to improve the situation of the elderly in Norway.

In the same way, attention is gradually being directed towards the special needs of the physically handicapped in the form of the construction of new buildings, planning of new living centres, etc. The organisations which represent the interests of the handicapped, play an important role as pressure groups with regard to the authorities. Integration of the physically handicapped into the normal society has altogether become a byword of all the social and cultural activities. An important milestone in this development is represented by the new Primary School Act which has as its objective the integration of the physically handicapped into the ordinary schools.

Of great significance to the overall assistance given to the handicapped is the work carried out by voluntary, humanitarian and the handicapped people's own organisations. During the last couple of years the authorities and these organisations have discussed cooperation with regard to coordinating social tasks on several occasions, especially with regard to measures aimed at well-being and increased contact on the local level.

SOCIAL CARE

The development of the social security system which we have in Norway has seen the concentration by society on the building up of social aspects of the system and the health service. The different forms of support cover most of the economic needs today. What is paid by social assistance is a modest sum compared with the enormous amounts which are paid via the State security budgets for the elderly, sick, disabled, unemployed and bereaved dependents. The development of the security and health sectors has meant that the municipal social service has been relieved of much of the burden and responsibility it had earlier.

The principal legislation which

covers the responsibilities and duties of the social service consists of: the Social Care Act, the Child Welfare Act and the Temperence Welfare Act. It is characteristic of the social sector that the responsibility and the administration of this work is accorded popularly voted committees. There shall be, in each municipality, a Social Committee, a Child Welfare Committee and a Temperance Committee. The Social Committee is the central organ within the municipality for the administration and coordination of the work in the social sector. As a general rule it may be said that the expenses incurred by the social sector are borne by the municipality. But the municipalities have, to a large extent, sought to aid those in difficulties via measures which may be financed through the national insurance scheme or other State financing instances. What form the aid is to take is assumed to be agreed in close consultation with the client. Help towards self-help is the principal aim of social care, while counsel and advice in crisis situations are important means whereby this may be achieved.

Social assistance has gradually assumed the character of temporary and supplementary economic aid. Even though it has been emphasised during all the postwar years that social care, like the social benefits, is a right, there is still a certain built-in reluctance on the part of some people to apply to a social office. It has proved difficult to alter attitudes in the population from a time when it was considered humiliating to accept help from the social service.

Norway is a country with a large consumption of social services. A steadily increasing proportion of the gross national income is used in connection with the requirements of the social and health sectors. Between 40 and 50 per cent of the combined appropriations of the State, social security and municipal budgets are now directed at different social measures.

Preventive Social Work

The Norwegian authorities will, in the coming years, pay greater attention to the prevention of social and health problems by, inter alia, seeking out and charting the correlations between these and social consideration must be taken in all areas of social planning.

The social problems which face young people have shown an increasing tendency in Norway during recent years, and the authorities are therefore studying several areas whereby this development may be contained. A number of resolutions have been adopted in recent years which are designed to strengthen the development possibilities for children. The municipalities are now required to build day institutions (nurseries) and health clinics for mothers and children. The new Abortion Act has, among other things, introduced social conditions as an independent factor for consideration with regard to abortion. Generally speaking family policy is undergoing reform and work is in hand in respect of measures for improving the economy of the family with children, the married woman's possibility of gainful employment, and different types of aid measures for families. The situation of the single provider has also been the subject of official reports. In recent years the authorities have launched comprehensive campaigns against intoxicating agents in order to create greater awareness of the problem inherent in alcohol and drugs, especially with regard to the young.

One complaint against the social service in Norway is that clients who seek assistance have often not known where to apply, and another is that the aid machinery is so split up. The social help which can be offered may also, to a certain degree, vary according to the part of the country in which one lives. The municipalities in Norway are of widely differing sizes with disparate economic expectations. The authorities will aim at a higher priority being accorded to the social services in the coming years, such as Child and Youth Welfare, Family Policy, Temperance Welfare and Social Care, than for the continued growth of the general benefits.

The strengthening of the municipalities' ability to provide social services will be to the advantage of all groups in the society. By no means least, a strengthening of social care will afford greater possibilities for increased help to the aged. There has been considerable emphasis placed on the improvement of their general situation in recent years, e.g. by means of rent subsidies, home help arrangements, subsidies for telephones and various general measures designed to improve their well being.

It has gradually become clear that the social administration and the service machinery do not possess sufficient resources whereby most people may receive adequate help. There is a serious lack of social and health personnel, a lack which has created great problems for social work in all the postwar years.

Unfortunately, it is not the case that a welfare society is a problem-free society. Even though a tremendous development has occured, new problems have also arisen which, among other things, are connected with the violent changes which have taken place in many social spheres since the second world war. The changes have been particularly noticeable with regard to the commercial, employment and demographic patterns. Significant alterations have been made with regard to age breakdown and family structure. The oil discoveries off the coast of Norway and the activities which have ensued in this connection, have increased the readjustment problems of the Norwegian society during the last few years.

The work of large groups of people has gradually become more monotonous. A high tempo is enforced at work and competition in employment has become sharper, pushing the weak to one side. The mortality rate has increased for some diseases — especially in the case of cardiorascular ailments and tumours, and traffic accidents. Mental disturbances have become more widespread. The increase in the consumption of tobacco, alcohol and, to some extent, drugs, is disquieting, even though we have managed to keep this consumption under a certain degree of control by means of legislation.

All the same it must be stated that Norway belongs among those countries of the world which are best endowed, both in terms of health and economy, and has the additional blessing of limitless natural treasures to bestow.

The economic expansion is today regarded, not as an isolated phenomenon, but as a stage in the overall aim of creating the greatest human security and wellbeing commensurate with preventing and decreasing the health and social problems. There must be a balance maintained between social policy development and economic growth.

The Education System in Norway

The Norwegian education system is an official responsibility, even though there are a number of private schools which are run at different levels. The apportionment of responsibility is such that the municipalities have the main responsibility for the obligatory teaching in the primary school, which in Norway lasts for 9 years. The counties are responsible for further education (10th—12th grades), while the State is responsible for higher education (universities, colleges, etc.). The State, however, also affords considerable support towards the running and building of primary schools and further education schools. Private schools are also afforded assistance by the State and the counties in accordance with a special law. Officially administered schooling is free for pupils and students, although the private schools require tuition fees in the majority of cases. Comprehensive supportive arrangements have been established for pupils and students in order to avoid discriminatory treatment as a result of social and geographical differences.

Nurseries

A number of Norwegian children receive their first education at nurseries. Such institutions are run by municipalities, private organisations, companies etc., often with support from the municipality and State. The nurseries offer pedagogically oriented activities primarily for children between 3 and 6 years. There is a great shortage of nursery places, even though a considerable number of new nurseries have been built during recent years. The nurseries do not constitute an integral part of the education system.

THE PRIMARY SCHOOL

A child commences primary school during the year it attains 7 years of age. In 1969 nine years compulsory schooling was introduced via legislation for all children in the country, and this has been carried out since 1973/74. Physically handicapped children have also been given the right to schooling within the ordinary primary school since 1976. The objective is for the physically handicapped to receive their education within their normal local environment. There will, however, continue to be special schools available for those who would benefit most from them.

Norway has had 7 years obligatory schooling at the primary school level since 1889. The schooling policy of this century has been directed at the building up of a type of school which affords all children the same general education, and which may constitute a basis for all further education.

The primary school is currently organised as a six-year lower stage school and a three-year upper stage school, with the availability of a voluntary tenth school year. The yearly intakes are about 60 000 pupils, so that the total number of pupils attending primary schools is about 580 000. Teaching at the upper stage level is organised so that there is some choice of subjects during the last two years. The teaching schedules specify subject and teaching time apportionment for the individual class levels, and provide frameworks for the working material. At the same time the plan affords the individual school and teacher freedom of choice within the frameworks, besides responsibility for the pedagogic presentation.

The primary school is organised into school districts within the individual municipalities, so that the geographic catchment area constitutes a district. There are c. 2 000 districts in the country. The most usual school size at the lower stage level is one class for each year. The maximum number of pupils per class is 30, while the average is just over 20 pupils. At the lower stage level Norway has a decentralised school structure with relatively many small school units. About 1 000 schools do not have all the school years in their own classes. In some districts all the years are concentrated in a single class. At the upper stage level the schools are usually larger, with two or three parallel classes. Here also, the maximum number of pupils per class is 30, while the average is under 25 per class.

In order to achieve the desired range of availability of optional subjects at the upper stage school, the schools have to be of a certain size, although new schools are not designed for more than 600 pupils.

The municipal authorities have complete responsibility for the development and management of the primary schools. Each municipality has a school board, which is politically constituted in order to reflect the individual parties' representation on the municipal council. The school board manages the schools which the municipality operates, appoints teachers, etc.

In order to ensure the coordination of primary school development in the municipalities, a school director is appointed for each county. He is the representative of the State and is a point of contact between the Ministry and the individual municipalities. The Ministry of Church and Education is the ultimate administrative authority. A separate advisory organ, The Basic School Council, aids the Ministry in its work with the primary school's pedagogic development.

Expenses connected with the primary school are covered by municipal budgets, but the State contributes fairly considerable amounts towards teaching costs and investments.

UPPER SECONDARY SCHOOLS

Norway is currently involved in carrying out comprehensive reforms affecting the upper secondary school (10th—12th grades). The reforms are aimed at a coordination of general subject and vocational subject education, which has previously taken place in different types of schools, affording the pupils the possibility of a free choice within the range provided by the upper secondary school. The difficulties which have so far obtained with regard to the changeover between the different types of school, will now be overcome.

Norway has hitherto had a number of different types of schools which were all based upon completion of primary school: upper stage with different lines, vocational schools for crafts and industry, commercial schools, domestic schools, maritime schools and fishery schools.

The new Upper Secondary School Act which was passed in 1974 and put into effect in 1976, merges all these school types together into one common upper secondary school system. The reform will have been carried out in its entirety by 1980. It is being introduced following comprehensive trials at upper stage and vocational training schools during a number of years.

At present there are altogether c. 130 000 places in further education. The aim is to build up the capacity by c. 5 000 new places each year, so that it will be possible to provide those who complete primary school with the right to three years' further education.

The teaching choice will now be made available through **lines of study** in the combined upper secondary school, and the following lines of study are available:

General subjects
Home crafts and aesthetic subjects
Fishery and shipping subjects
Sports subjects
Commercial subjects
Domestic subjects
Handcraft and industrial subjects
Social and health subjects

In addition there is agricultural education which is not yet covered by the new Act. **Folk High School** (see p. 71) are also excluded from the new Act at present.

Pupils in a general subject line of study, which is the closest equivalent of the earlier upper secondary school (gymnas), choose certain basic subjects besides individual optional subjects of particular interest. During the second and third years the pupils are able to choose an intensification or specialisation within different lines: Natural Science line, Sociology line, Language line. Certain minimum requirements are stipulated with regard to subject combinations within the three lines. A three-year further education will usually (dependent upon subject and course combinations) afford general study competence in respect of higher education.

The counties have had the responsibility for the building and management of most upper secondary schools since 1964. A separate **county school board** is responsible for the upper secondary schools within the county. The board is politically constituted, in the same way as the municipal school boards.

The ultimate administrative organ is the Ministry of Church and

Education. A professional instance has been established under the Ministry, the Council for Further Education, with a number of sub-committees which assist the Ministry with regard to professional and pedagogic questions.

The State also grants aid with regard to the building and management of upper secondary schools. The degree of aid varies, according to the economy of the individual county, from 30 to 75%.

In the case of private upper secondary schools the State covers between 50 and 75% of certain regular expenses.

In further education too, there are opportunities for the integration of physically handicapped pupils in the normal teaching. Pupils who are accepted, and who are deemed to need special assistance as a result of an expert assessment, may receive more than 3 years' tuition. As far as it is possible, all pupils are to be taught in the ordinary school.

THE FOLK HIGH SCHOOLS

must be regarded as a typically Nordic type of school with long and characteristic traditions. They have their origin in the philosophy of the Age of Enlightenment, and the first schools were established in Denmark during the last century by the wellknown hymnist and author, N. Grundtvig. The idea spread rapidly over the whole of Scandinavia, and there are today c. 100 schools of this type with about 8 000 pupils in Norway alone.

The folk high schools offer general education tuition for young adults, and are subject to a special Act. There are no examinations at these schools, and they are relatively free with regard to the school system and teaching presentation. The folk high schools are boarding schools, and there is

great emphasis placed on the social interchanges between the teachers and the pupils during their free time. These will probably retain their present status irrespective of the Act regarding further education, for some years to come.

HIGHER EDUCATION

By Higher Education is meant all types of education over and above the upper secondary school level. The education institutions in higher education in Norway constitute a diffuse group both with regard to the type of education available, the type of teaching and the administrative structure. The universities and the scientific colleges occupy a leading position within higher education.

Originally all post-upper stage education was available at the so-called academic seats of learning. All the academic institutions have the dual objective of educating graduates and carrying out research within various subject areas. The need for highly qualified experts in a steadily increasing number of areas has gradually broken the monopoly situation of the academic institutions.

The organisation of higher education in Norway is currently under revision, and at the same time efforts are being made to increase the combined capacity from c. 60 000 places at present (of which 33 000 are at the universities) to 80 000 towards the end of the 1980's.

About 15% of the students are engaged in post-graduate studies. Some 3 000 Norwegians study at overseas seats of learning. Norway has about 1 550 overseas students.

The majority of lectures are held in Norwegian, and a large proportion of the text books are Norwegian. The intake of the various studies is often limited (especially medicine, odontology and engineering subjects). Those foreigners who are interested in studying in Norway are advised to contact the particular institute which is of interest in order to be furnished with detailed informative material regarding intake requirements, financing and the possibilities of studying in Norway.

The vast majority of higher education institutes are completely financed via State means, which are granted by the Storting. The private higher education institutes also receive aid. Private institutions are to be found within technical and economic education, among others. There is also an independent theological faculty. The universities enjoy a traditional freedom of determining the contents of their curricula with regard to examinations and scientific degrees. The right to hold examinations and issue degrees is granted by the King in pursuance of the law. The Ministry stipulates the professional requirements with regard to teacher training.

The four universities in Norway provide education which leads to a first degree (cand. mag.) and higher degrees (cand. real., cand. philol., cand. jur., cand. med., etc.). The course leading to a first degree normally takes between 4 and $4^1/_2$ years, and that leading to a higher degree between 6 and 8 years.

The course which aims at a first university degree (cand. mag.) is usually divided into a basic subject (1 year) and two intermediary subjects ($1^1/_2$ years each). In order to attain a higher degree, one of the intermediary subjects is extended to a major subject (2—3 years).

The university year in Norway is split into two, with a Spring Term (15.1.—15.6.) and an Autumn Term (20.8.—20.12.).

The autonomy of the universities and the scientific colleges also applies to the economic situation to a great extent, even though the Storting imposes relatively detailed frameworks when approving the university budgets.

The administration of the universities varies. What is common, however, is the fact that all types of employees and students are represented on the decision-making instances. No one has a place on such an instance without having been elected. The student representation on various organs at different universities varies from 15 to 50% (in studies committees), and up to 30% in the higher instances. As is the case with other Norwegian higher education institutes, teachers of lecturer status and above are established.

UNIVERSITIES AND SCIENTIFIC COLLEGES

The University of Oslo

is the country's oldest and largest university. In 1977 it had 20 000 students and about 3 000 employees. It was founded in 1811 and commenced its activities in 1833. Up until 1946 it was the only university in the country. There are altogether 7 faculties at this university which cover all the traditional university subjects; the faculties of theology, law, medicine, mathematics and natural sciences, history and philosophy, sociology and odontology.

There is also an International Summer School at the University of Oslo. Every year there are about 250 students from all the corners of the earth attending. Tuition is conducted in English and provides an introduction to Norwegian social conditions. Information regarding intake requirements, financing etc. will be supplied by the school upon request.

The University of Bergen

was founded in 1946, and currently totals c. 8 000 students and c. 1 500 employees. The university holds degree examinations in medicine, odontology, law, scientific subjects, the humanities and sociological subjects.

The University of Trondheim

was founded in 1969, and is based on the Teaching College of Norway, (founded 1922) a scientific museum (The Royal Norwegian Scientific Society's Museum) and the Norwegian Institute of Technology (NTH). A choice of studies has been developed on the basis of the teaching college, within the following disciplines: scientific subjects, the humanities and sociological subjects. In addition there is tuition in medicine (at present only the clinical part of the course). Apart from the NTH there are about 3 500 students and 300 employees in Trondheim.

The Norwegian Institute of Technology (NTH)

was founded in 1910, and had c. 4 700 students in 1976, together with c. 1 200 employees. The college is the only instance which trains civil engineers in Norway, and it provides examination in mining, construction, electrical engineering subjects, chemistry, mechanical engineering subjects and applied physics. The course of study is normally 4—5 years. The college also has an architectural department.

The University of Trondheim is currently involved in a comprehensive development programme.

The University of Tromsø

was founded in 1969, and had its first student intake in 1972. It now has 1 500 students and about 550 employees, of which half are teaching staff. It affords examinations in medicine, scientific subjects, the humanities, fishery subjects and sociological subjects. The organisational structure differs from that of the other universities.

Towards the end of the 19th, and at the beginning of the 20th century, independent specialist colleges were established to cater for new, professionally oriented academic education. The Norwegian Institute of Technology has already been mentioned.

The Agricultural University of Norway (NLH)

at Ås near Oslo, was founded in 1897, and is concerned with research and education in agriculture, horticulture ,forestry, dairying and land re-allocation.

The Norwegian Veterinary College

in Oslo was established in 1935. The course lasts 6 years. The college has a good 200 students.

The Norwegian School of Economics and Business Administration

of Bergen, was established in 1936 and trains economists. The college examines in business and social economics, jurisprudence and administration. The training normally takes 4 years. The college has c. 1 200 students and c. 180 employees.

The Architectural College of Oslo

was permanently founded in 1961. The college trains architects along the same lines as the Norwegian Institute of Technology. The normal course of study last $4^{1}/_{2}$ years. The college has over 200 students.

The Norwegian College of Physical Education

Oslo, was founded in 1968. The

college is designed for up to 300 students. Basic, intermediary and major subject examinations may be taken in physical education. The training equips one for, among other things, teaching physical training at schools.

The State Academy of Art

Oslo, was founded in 1909, and trains graphic artists, painters and sculptors. The course is normally 4 years.

The State Academy of Music

Oslo, was founded in 1972, and trains performing musicians and composers.

The Norwegian College of Fishery

was founded in 1972, and is an 'umbrella organisation' for fishery education which is given at the universities in Tromsø, Trondheim and Bergen, besides the Norwegian School of Economics and Business Administration.

THE REGIONAL HIGH SCHOOL SYSTEM

— will gradually include all the educational institutes which provide occupational oriented 2—3 year higher education. The regions equate with the counties, and in each county there is a **Regional High School Board.** The board consists of a majority of representatives appointed by the Ministry on the recommendation of the county, and representatives from among the employees and the students at the high schools. The regional high school board expresses itself with regard to the question of priority in respect of different high schools in its region, and is responsible for the planning of higher education in the region. The individual high school has its

own internal administrative organ which, among other things, is responsible for the professional aspects. The financial means are earmarked for the individual high school by the State, to a large extent.

The Regional Colleges

started in 1969, and now offer tuition at high school level in 10 counties. The training covers a wide range of subjects which are principally vocationally oriented, but which also fit in well with a further education context. A wide range of disciplines are taught within social subjects, the humanities and the technical and natural science subjects. The forms of study and examinations vary, and are suited to the individual course's content and object. Study opportunities are also available to part-time students. The examination at the conclusion of the 2 and 3 year courses grants the right to the title of Regional College graduate. The regional colleges are also involved in research with the main emphasis on local and regional problems.

The Pedagogic High Schools

(Teacher Training Colleges) train teachers for pre-schools, primary and secondary schools, and provide further education for these. Norway has 29 pedagogic high schools, with a total of 11 000 full-time students. Teacher training lasts 3 years. The pedagogic high schools also provide pedagogic training for university graduates and vocational teachers.

Teachers in further education will normally have a university degree, or comprehensive professional background.

Engineering High Schools

(previously technical schools) train engineers within the traditional disciplines of building and construction, electro-technology, chemical technology and mechanical technology, which again affords a varied choice of courses of study. Training lasts for 2 years usually. The examination from the engineering high school affords professional competence first and foremost, besides competence for further studies.

Handicraft schools

give training in art and arts and crafts, for between 3 and 4 years.

ADULT EDUCATION

Great emphasis has been placed upon adult education during recent years in Norway. A new Act governing adult education became operative on 1.8.77. This states that the responsibility for adult education which is aimed at official examinations devolves upon the official school system at the respective levels. Individual committees have been formed in each municipality and county with regard to adult education. The responsibility for other forms of adult education is placed with the voluntary information organisations. These are administered partly by political organisations, partly by interest groups, and they arise partly out of university environments, etc. The responsibility for alternative forms of adult education is shared between the official school system (i.e. municipalities, counties and the State) and the organisations. In 1977 the State provided 128 million kroner for adult education.

Adult education in Norway has long traditions, with a basis in the people's information organisations. By means of the adult education measures it will be possible to even out the educational inequality between the younger age groups and that part of the population which has not had more than the 7 years of primary school.

Education via correspondence receives its own appropriations in Norway, and constitutes an important part of adult education. The State supports correspondence schools by means of grants. Teaching via correspondence is carried out partly by correspondence schools and partly by the organisations as a feature of their information work. The military services also conduct comprehensive training programmes in civilian subjects. The ultimate authority for adult education rests with the Ministry of Church and Education.

WELFARE AND STUDY FINANCING

The financing of studies is conducted through the offices of the Government Loan Fund for Education, which assists school pupils and students with regard to all kinds of education which lasts for at least one year. Support is granted partly through stipends, and partly via loans. In principle, pupils at upper secondary schools are given stipends, and students in higher education both stipends and loans. Loans are not subject to a means test, but are accorded within a scale based on the costs of the individual courses of study. Loans are also made available for students who study half the day. Foreign students may, subject to certain conditions, be granted a study loan, as long as it is designed for studies within Norway. The loans are repayable over a 10—15 year period.

The State also provides substantial grants in respect of welfare work among pupils and students (canteen management, student accommodation, etc.). The total grants towards social measures for pupils and students during 1977 amounted to 473 million kroner.

Science and Research

Norway spends about 1.3 per cent of its Gross National Product on research and development. In 1974 the figure was approx. 1.6 thousand million kroner, of which 61 per cent came from public funds either as direct grants to research from the central government or from proceeds of the State Football Pool, which are divided between research and efforts to promote sporting activities. Fifty per cent of the public funds went directly to the universities and colleges, mainly from the budget of the Ministry of Church and Education. The university research institutes are responsible for all of 80 per cent of the basic research done in Norway. A further 35 per cent of public funds went to finance research at Government laboratories or institutes, most of which are specialized research institutes attached to one of the Ministries, such as the Institute of Marine Research under the Ministry of Fisheries and the Institute of Occupational Health under the Ministry of Local Government and Labour.

Sectors of Research

As in all industrialized countries, a large proportion of the money spent on research goes to engineering and technology, but recent years have shown a relative increase in the amounts made available for agricultural technology, the humanities and the social sciences.

The Research Councils

There are four research councils in Norway. Three of them, the Agricultural Research Council of Norway (NLVF), the Norwegian

Total Expenditure on Research and Development by Fields of Science, 1974.*

	Million Nkr.	%
Humanities	80.0	5
Social Sciences .	124.2	7
Natural Sciences .	185.0	11
Medical Science .	178.8	11
Veterinary Science	17.1	1
Agricultural Technology	92.3	6
Engineering and Technology	966.1	59
Total	1643.5	100

* R + D Statistics 1974.

Research Council for Science and the Humanities (NAVF) and the Royal Norwegian Council for Scientific and Industrial Research (NTNF), were established soon after the second world war to promote and coordinate activities in their respective fields of interest and to ensure that research results are used for the benefit of the country. They stimulate recruitment to research through fellowship programmes and give grants to research activities at the universities. The Norwegian Fisheries Research Council was organized in 1972 to take care of special problems relating to Norway's extensive fishing industry.

Special Fields of Interest

Norway's geographical position and far-flung coastline bounding on an ocean full of natural resources have led to a natural interest in arctic research, studies of the Northern Lights, oceanography, marine biology and meteorology. Norwegian scientists have made important contributions to the knowledge of ocean currents and annual migrations of fish. Vilhelm

Bjerknes was one of the creators of modern meteorology. There is also a strong archeological tradition in Norway. Excavations of the Oseberg and Gogstad viking ships have led to a better understanding of the ancient Norwegian peoples, and recent investigations at Bryggen in Bergen have brought to light many interesting finds from the Middle Ages.

Current Trends

The present emphasis seems to be on problems directly affecting modern society — pollution, protection of the environment and natural resources, and studies of social welfare. The Ministry of the Environment, NTNF and NLVF are collaborating on a project intended to determine the effect of acid precipitation from Western Europe on life in Norwegian lakes and rivers, and the same ministry, together with NAVF, NTNF and NFFR has initiated an extensive monitoring of pollution in the North Sea. A recent important step is the proposal to establish a Council for Research for Societal Planning within the NAVF organization, with a strong representation of user groups, and where the aim is to coordinate problem-oriented interdisciplinary research on the large problem complexes associated with long-term planning in all sectors of society.

Culture

Decentralisation and democratisation of the cultural amenities are the key words in the context of Norwegian cultural policy. This means that as many as possible will be able to avail themselves of the cultural amenities.

The creative urge is a fundamental human trait. This is why it has become a political objective in modern societies to create the right conditions for such activities.

The State has produced three publications which are to constitute the cornerstones of Norwegian cultural life in the future:

Two cultural reports concern themselves with the actual organisation and financing of cultural work. In a supplement, they outline the principles of a «new cultural policy». An artists report deals with the relationship between the artist and the society.

Norwegian cultural life is currently characterised by the debate surrounding the contents of these reports, both positively and negatively.

Nonetheless it is a fact that Norway is far to the fore in an international context with regard to the drawing up of lines in the relationship between the artist and the society of which he/she is a part and in which he/she functions.

LANGUAGE

Norway has a good four million inhabitants. The majority of these understand each other's everyday language. One exception is the Lapps, a small group of people who mostly live in North Norway. These have their own language which belongs to the Finno-Ugric language group.

In spite of the low population, Norway has two parallel language forms: Bokmål and Nynorsk. Both of these are closely related to the other Scandinavian languages.

Up until the end of the 19th century, Norway had one official language: Riksmål. This had been strongly influenced by the fact that Norway had more or less been subservient to Denmark. Round about 1850 a new Norwegian language was created which was based on dialects. This formed the basis for making the language more purely Norwegian. The new language was given the name «Landsmål».

Today both the official languages have developed further from their origins, and they have also been given new names: Riksmål has become Bokmål, while Landsmål is today known as Nynorsk (new Norwegian). The languages are given equal status in official usage and in the schools.

LITERATURE

Present-day Norwegian literature features several names, and is actively engaged by contemporary considerations. The second world war brought about a fundamental cleft in the country's history, and this is reflected in the prominent authors who have been active since 1945.

The German occupation involved a literary constriction. Literary production dried up; the Nazis controlled the publishing houses.

After the liberation, literature bloomed again — as never before. It was mainly war novels and adventure stories from the war years, which came first. Most of them were seven-day wonders, even though a few have stood the test of time.

But Norwegian literature moved quite quickly away from the optimism of the joys of liberation, to intellectual despair and pessimism. At the same time book production sank to the prewar level again. The poetry of the age became introverted and subjective, thematically centred on the concepts of fear and weakness. In the fields of prose, the novel blossomed.

Attempts were made to express the fear of destruction in a sparse form, via allegory, symbolism and experiments.

Interest swung round in the latter half of the 1950's. Then it was the recent past which became the theme. The result was a form of literature with a broader epic form and without experimentation.

In spite of the interest in the recent past, the present day is also characterised by disintegration. But the past is simple and the future problematic. One soon sees the results of alien feeling and suspicion of the absurd in a social and development context, crystallising itself in literature which centres around the problem of identity.

Well into the 1960's came the reaction to the change from the parochial situation to the consumer society. A wave of social criticism built up. The concepts of neutrality and objectivity assumed a suspicious tone. The byword became «Everything is politics».

Viewed economically, literature was in a weak position in the 1960's. Most Norwegian books represented losses for the publishers. The State's offer to authors consisted of 3-year working grants. From 1956 the Norwegian Cultural Fund began to buy 1000 copies of all Norwegian literary works and distribute them among the libraries. This support has meant that Norwegian authors enjoy generally better conditions than their colleagues in other countries, and literature is now in a new era of prosperity.

It may be said generally that Norwegian writing since 1965 has undergone a development which has taken far longer in other countries.

But Norwegian literature does not only stem from the present day. Our literary roots are to be found in the Edda writings. These are Norway's oldest literary documents (probably from the 9th or 10th century A.D.)

Norwegian literary traditions survived through the centuries by means of verbal recounting of adventures and folktales.

After the dissolution of the Union with Denmark in 1814, Henrik Wergeland, with his visionary romantic poetry, created a name for himself as Norway's greatest poet. He heralded a Norwegian literary renaissance.

The time was ripe for what has been called the golden age of literature. The first who attained international acclaim was Bjørnstjerne Bjørnson. Like Wergeland, he started out on a nationalistic basis, but developed through his dramas and short stories to become a modern realist.

Henrik Ibsen, on the other hand, turned himself inwards, and concerned himself through a long authorship mainly with ethical questions. Together with the realists Jonas Lie and Alexander Kielland, Bjørnson and Ibsen are called the «Big Four» of Norwegian literature. However, they were by no means alone in creating the Golden Age. This honour must also be shared with Arne Garborg and some of those who followed behind. Among these are the creators of the lyrical style in Norwegian literature: Hans E. Kinck and Knut Hamsun. Bjørnson, Hamsun and Sigrid Undset have all received the Nobel Prize for Literature.

THEATRE

One of the aims of Norwegian cultural policy is to bring the theatre out to as many of the country's inhabitants as possible.

Because of the country's topography, the population is spread over wide areas, and travelling theatres which have been able to produce their plays on improvised stages (meeting houses, etc.) have been the only theatrical amenity available to rural districts for many years. After the second world war the **Riksteatret** was founded with the object of covering the whole country. Even though Riksteatret is State-administered and subsidised by as much as 18.6 million kroner a year, it has not proved possible to cover the whole country satisfactorily.

One of the main aims of the Norwegian theatre world, therefore, is the building up of **Regional Theatres.** These are to function as independent theatre companies, and be responsible for part of the touring activity which was previously carried out by the Riksteatret. So far six such regional theatres have been established and the results to date are in favour of further developments along these lines.

These six theatres are: Tromsø (Hålogaland Teater), Trondheim (Trøndelag Teater), Molde (The Regional Theatre of Møre og Romsdal), Skien (Telemark Teater), Stavanger (Rogaland Teater) and Førde (The Regional Theatre of Sogn og Fjordane).

But Norwegian theatre does not only consist of the future and development. The country's first permanent theatre was opened in Oslo in 1827, with Bergen gaining its first regular theatre in 1850.

The National Theatre in Oslo was completed in 1899, and has been the country's principal theatre since that time. Together with Den Nationale Scene in Bergen, these two theatres have had enormous significance for Norwegian theatre. Many of Norway's most prominant actors began their career at Den Nationale Scene. Two smaller towns

— Halden and Drammen — also gained their own theatres at an early stage.

Two other factors exercised considerable influence on Norwegian theatre, namely the two dramatists Ibsen and Bjørnson. They both served as inspiring theatre managers at the same time as being active writers, producing several plays.

Today Oslo has three theatres with main and subsidiary auditoria. Apart from the National Theatre there is Det Norske Teatret which stages productions with Nynorsk dialogue only, and Oslo Nye Teater. Apart from regular TV theatre one evening a week, a number of Nordic series and Sunday matinees are transmitted by TV.

Seven of Norway's theatres (two in Oslo) are subsidised equally by the Government and the respective municipalities. Government subsidies to theatres amounted to 74.2 million kroner in 1977.

OPERA

While major opera houses throughout the world are experiencing a diminishing public interest, there is an increase in the support for opera and ballet to be discerned in Norway. The opera's travelling performances — one of the constituents of a policy of decentralised cultural amenities — almost always play to packed houses during their tours of the country.

Den Norske Opera was founded in 1958. The intention was that it should be both an opera and ballet institution, where both artistic media were equal. In addition it was to act as an opera for the whole country — a national opera — but with its headquarters in Oslo. The world-famous singer Kirsten Flagstad was the first

administrator of the opera company.

The opera company is owned and administered by the State and the Oslo Municipal Council together. These provide 60% and 40% respectively of the necessary subsidies, which in 1977 totalled about 36.5 million kroner.

MUSIC

Norwegian music is currently in the midst of a very fruitful period. However, one does not have to go far beyond the country's borders to discover that for most people Norwegian music is practically synonymous with Edvard Grieg. The further away from Norway one gets, the stronger this association becomes.

Since Grieg's death in 1907 there has been a constant development within music. Young talented musicians took up Grieg's legacy, found inspiration in his works — and progressed further. Grieg's national romanticism had to give way to a general, realistic romanticism. The leading exponent of this in Norway was Christian Sinding.

Real modernism appeared in our own century. Fartein Valen was the first Norwegian composer who espoused modernism.

Up to the present day, for reasons of simplicity, it is possible to divide Norwegian composers into four groups; the nationalists, the national-radicals, the moderate modernist and the futurists/avant-gardists. Leading nationalists were Arne Eggen and David Monrad Johansen. Eivind Groven is to be found on the extreme nationalist wing.

Bjarne Brustad belongs to the second group, the national-radicals. He aims at combining Norwegian and European traditions in his compositions. Two other inter-

Edvard Grieg (1843—1907).

posing colleagues include: **Alfred Janson, Kåre Kolberg** and **Folke Strømholm**. Other known composers are: Conrad Baden, Finn Mortensen, Edvard Fliflet Bræin, Hallvard Johnsen, Knut Nystedt, Geirr Tveit and Sparre Olsen.

On the one hand, therefore, Grieg gave rise to a musical acceleration in Norway. On the other hand he was preceeded by other signficant composers, and he was by no means the only composer of stature.

Of those who perhaps gained greatest prominence alongside Grieg, was Johan Svendsen. The two complemented each other: while Grieg supplied musical pearls of an intimate form, Svendsen provided us with weighty compositions on the symphonic plane. Together they fulfilled the promise of Rikard Nordraak of Norwegian classical music founded on folk music. Johan Halvorsen followed the lead of Svendsen and Grieg, and might almost be regarded as being a classical romanticist.

The best-known of the musical generation before this, were Ole Bull and Halfdan Kjerulf. Ole Bull was the first musician to gain world repute as a virtuoso violinist.

Norwegians are very interested in music. Orchestras, choirs and bands are formed even in rural districts and small towns. A number of guest musicians and singers contribute to interesting concert seasons.

International summer festivals are held annually in Bergen, and jazz festivals in Molde and Kongsberg.

Four orchestras (in Oslo, Bergen, Trondheim and Stavanger) receive Government and municipal subsidies as well as regular fees from the Norwegian Broadcasting Corporation.

The Rikskonsertene maintain touring activities and are the principle providers of music to provincial Norway.

esting composers in this category are Harald Sæverud and Klaus Egge. Both of these are prominent figures in contemporary Norwegian music life. Sæverud started out as an internationalist, and during and after the war years, has observed the possibilities inherent in typical Norwegian music. His colleague Klaus Egge has created his music on a national basis and, at the same time, oriented himself with regard to contemporary music.

The group moderate modernists includes Pauline Hall. She was a representative of the revolt against the traditions of Norwegian music. Bjørn Fongaard followed in her wake, with his search for complete freedom of expression, as well as Antonio Bibalo who also strove towards freedom of expression and avoidance of musical dogma.

Perhaps the best-known from among the last group, futurists/avant-gardists, is Arne Nordheim, one of the young trail-blazers in Norwegian music today. He has already produced a number of varied, fascinating works. His com-

FILM

Norwegian films are undergoing strong growth. About 10 feature films and as many as 80 short films are produced annually.

As a rule the films are designed for the domestic market and the film-makers have had to rely on State subsidies. A black and white film is subsidised to the extent of 45% of gross box office receipts. A colour film or other more expensive production receives 55% of production costs. In addition, producers may apply for a State guarantee covering 80—90% of production costs. Special guarantees are also forthcoming in respect of short films, documentaries, educational films and experimental and childrens films.

All the films which are shown publicly in Norway must first be approved by the State Film Control.

There has been considerable discussion surrounding the censorship of films.

During the course of the years, the Film Control has become more liberal, but is still considerably stricter than in neighbouring Sweden and Denmark.

ART

The monumental work of art occupies a prominent place in Norwegian art. The new direction, including the purely motif-oriented, came about towards the end of the 50's. It was the abstract painting which caught on here, as it did elsewhere in Scandinavia.

One of the first major works which was undertaken in the new idiom was the joint work of Inger Sitter and Carl Nesjar in connection with the Government building in Oslo in 1956. A whole wall in sand-blown natural concrete shows an abstract theme of monumental dimensions.

Edvard Munch (1863-1944).

Otherwise it might be said that the first 15—20 postwar years of Norwegian art were remarkably uneventful. The art historian, Magne Malmanger, has attempted to explain this by pointing to the strong position enjoyed by the painting of the between-war art, and the clear academic teaching.

The monumentality which was discernible during the between-war years, gave birth to a new blossoming in the 60's, but dogma was put to one side in favour of free experimentation.

During the 40's and 50's, most Norwegian painters expressed themselves via semi-abstraction.

Towards the end of the 50's abstract painting made a complete breaktrough. Beneath this there still lies an idea and a structure which stems from nature.

Among the younger painters is Jens Johannessen, who was initially involved in the spontaneous movement. Since then, however, he has evolved his own form, — a kind of rose-painting in a modern idiom — and in movement.

Nature, for Jakob Weidemann, is the end-all and be-all. His point of departure is to be found where he is standing. From this position he evolves his lyrical paintings. Frantz

King Haakon VII (1872-1957). Statue by Nils Aas in 7. juni-plass in Oslo.

Widerberg is one of the most interesting young painters in Norway today and works with a kind of fantastic abstract figuratism.

These artists are all inheritors of a long line of artistic personalities from ages past. In the 1800's, Johan Chr. Dahl and Thomas Fearnley breathed fresh air into Norwegian painting. They brought the continental romanticism home with them from their studies abroad, an idiom which was changed to a national romanticism by the following generation. The most prominent of these were Lars Hertervig, Christian Krohg, Erik Werenskiold and Fritz Thaulow.

The latter three were to exert considerable influence on Edvard Munch. Harriet Backer occupied a modest position during her lifetime, but is today regarded as one of the greatest painting talents which Norway has produced. Besides her, the central figures of this generation are the neoromanticist Harald Solberg and the painter Halfdan Egedius.

At the turn of the century the 'colour-poets' Oluf Wold Thorne and Thorvald Erichsen appeared, but the most famous of this generation was Edvard Munch. He has exerted influence upon many European artists and is regarded as one of the founders of expressionism. Today there is separate Edvard Munch Museum in Oslo where the greater part of his work is exhibited.

After him came painters such as Axel Revold, Per Krohg, Alf Rolfsen, who, together with Henrik Sørensen, were responsible for the majority of the murals in Oslo Town Hall (completed 1950).

Sculpture

After Carl Nesjar had completed his decoration of the Government building, he continued to create sculptures in sand-blown concrete.

He commenced cooperation with Pablo Picasso which resulted in large concrete sculptures in the Nordic countries, Europe and the USA.He later used metal in sculptures which would be covered by ice in winter, in a kind of frozen «fountain».

Odd Tandberg is another sculptor who has worked a lot with sand-blown concrete, in an abstract-figurative form. Arnold Haukeland also expresses himself in abstract forms, and he uses metal as his material.

Nils Aas occupies a leading place among the young sculptors. His sculpture is abstract in a concrete, architectural form where the figurative element in the motif is still preserved. One of his principal works is the Haakon VII statue in 7. juni-plassen in Oslo. Seen through international eyes, Gustav Vigeland is still the best-known Norwegian sculptor. His early works from the first two decades of the century, show his quality. In the great sculpture park at Frogner in Oslo, his works are, however, tinged with a hint of mannerism.

The **Riksgalleriet** was founded in 1952, with the objective of making art available to as many people in the country as possible. The gallery's touring exhibitions are well attended. Each year works of art are bought for the collection.

ARTS AND CRAFTS

The expression «Arts and Crafts» covers objects which have a practical as well as an artistic value. The Norwegian expression «brukskunst» was created in 1912 by Harry Fett. Since then it has been used and misused, but has become an irradicable concept in Scandinavian languages.

Even so, the concept is of even earlier origin. Few countries are able to point to a folk art which has flowered so richly, and with so many local varations, as in Norway.

To a large extent this is because of the privileged position enjoyed by the Norwegian farmers, compared with farmers in most other European countries. Norwegian folk art had its «golden-age» in the 1800's, with much help from the economic boom in the country at that time. It was as though age-old folk-art traditions came to full maturity. This is the basis on which Norwegian arts and crafts stand.

Today Norwegian arts and crafts are an export commodity which enjoys international renown and good quality.

The central organ for this cultural activity in Norway is the National Association of Norwegian Arts and Crafts.

The Ministry of Foreign Affairs gives constant support for the development of Norwegian arts and crafts via exhibition activities abroad.

ARCHITECTURE

Since 1950 there has evolved what we can call a modern, Norwegian architecture. It is characterised by strong influences from indigenous tradition, but also by international currents in our own age.

Perhaps one of the most remarkable aspects of Norwegian architectural history is the fact that a contemporary functionalism was developed at an early juncture. The modernists achieved a remarkable breadth in the 1930's.

However, after the second world war a new «national» reaction came about. The results were not always convincing, but reminded the internationalists of the regional conditions which the functionalists had ignored.

Norway is one of the northern-most populated countries in the world, and possibly the country which affords its inhabitants the most difficult topography.

4⁰/₀ of the country is cultivated while 75⁰/₀ consists of mountain areas. The country has a similar area to that of Italy and is covered by snow for nearly half the year. The population density is 12 per km² as opposed to 60 on average throughout the rest of Europe.

It is not easy to build in such a country. The region itself presents great problems. It is not possible to apply the modern international architecture's approach to the problem without further ado.

In the 19th century, Norway took part in the general continental architectural development. The historical use of various styles governed the architecture. The capital, Oslo, provides many reminders of this epoch. Large parts of the city are reminiscent of a German town of the 1800's.

Chr. H. Grosch fashioned his work on the German, Karl F. Schinkel, when he built the university and other official buildings.

Grosch, H. D. F. Linstow and Alexis de Chateauneuf were responsible for a number of monumental constructions during the 1850's.

Henrik Bull was the one who brought the historical movement in Norwegian architecture to an end. He led the various styles through to an admirable synthesis and combined the historical style with that of the Jugend school. He designed the National Theatre, the Historical Museum and the Government building, all of which date from the first year of the 1900's. Bull maintained contact with Europe, but the break came in 1905, the same year in which Norway gained her independence. A prevalent feature of Norwegian architectural history is the waves of nationalism, and in precisely that year a new wave arose which was characterised by its national romantic qualities, — not by the architectural ones.

Herman M. Schirmer was at the

Stave church at the Norwegian Folk Museum, Oslo.

forefront of this development. He was a senior lecturer at the School of Art and Crafts, and his pupils became exponents of the national trend.

Arnstein Arneberg was the one who combined the romantic style with our own national tradition, and was, together with Magnus Poulsson, the leading architect within the fashion.

Fr. Konow Lund was the first to reach beyond this national romanticism. In the same way as Frank Lloyd Wright, he found that architecture and nature are inseparably connected, and that Norwegian architecture should be suited to our difficult terrain. The reaction against romanticism began as a kind of abstract classicism. Pure functionalism came about later. Leading architects were Ove Bang and Arne Korsmo.

Among the most interesting names in Norwegian architecture are the instigators of the Franciscan monastry and St. Hallvard's Church in Oslo (both 1966), Kjell Lund and Nils Slaatto. In addition, architects such as Sverre Fehn and Geir Grung have produced excellent Norwegian architecture.

Norwegian architecture rests

upon solid roots. The most important Norwegian contribution to Middle Ages architecture was the stave churches. Originally there were a good 800, — today there are 30 more or less preserved.

There was, however, a rich stone architecture, and the cathedral in Trondheim is the largest and most important example. At the same time it is also the northernmost Gothic cathedral in the world — and the country's national shrine.

The oldest parts of the church are built in the Anglo-Norman style, dating back to c. 1150 A.D. The church was completed around 1320 A.D.

The largest profane Middle Ages building in stone is Håkonshallen (completed in 1260). There are otherwise relics of fine carpentry traditions to be found in several places.

The Rosenkrantz Tower in Bergen (c. 1580) and the Austråt and Rosendal manors (c. 1660) are the most important Norwegian buildings from the renaissance and baroque periods. In the 1700's wood was the predominant building material in Norwegian architecture. The prefect's residence in Trondheim is the finest example which has been preserved from that period, and it is the largest wooden building in the Nordic countries.

Government Support

The government finances or provides economic support for art galleries and exhibitions of plastic art, operas, orchestras, music festivals and academies, theatres, film production, public libraries, museums and archives.

The Norwegian Cultural Fund was established by a Parliamentary act of 1964 and has a consultative council of 13 members, appointed for a 4 years period. Grants to art and culture preservation are approved by the King on the advice of the Council, which will also have at its disposal sums for immediate support of projects or for its own initiatives. These decisions must be sanctioned by the Ministry of Church and Education.

The statutes originally provided that the yearly grants to the Fund should be at least a sum corresponding to the revenue of the purchase tax on periodicals and weeklies (introduced 1965, estimated at 15 mill. kroner). In 1967 purchase tax on weeklies and books was abolished. (By 1970 the new value-added tax was put on weeklies, not on books). But from 1967 the appropriations to the Fund are voted upon by Parliament independently of any revenue.

Government appropriations to the Fund in 1976 amount to 34 mill. kroner, covering approx. 9.3 mill. kroner to literature, 2.8 mill. kroner to music, 4.5 mill. kroner to pictorial art, 3.5 mill. kroner to culture preservation, 9.2 mill. kroner to buildings, and 4.8 mill. kroner to periodicals, reports, promotion of Lappish culture, film etc.

Other Allocations

Government grants to authors and artists are awarded in various forms:

1) **Life grants** 18 000 kroner (in 1977: 21 fellowships).
2) Honorary annuity (in 1977: 50 000).
3) **Grants for a 3 years' period:** 38 500 kroner (in 1977 : 100).
4) **Grants for a 3 years' period:** 10 000 kroner (in 1977 : 10).
5) **Scholarships for studies abroad:** (in 1977 : 17 à 20 000, 2 à 15 000, 15 à 12 000, 76 à 10 000 and 23 9000—4000 kroner).
6) **Scholarships for pictorial artists:** (in 1977 : 7 of 2000 kroner).
7) **Life grants for senior artists:** 9000 (in 1977 : 160). Total 1977: 8 449 000 kroner.

In addition, 6 616 000 kroner is granted in respect of 150 guaranteed artist incomes.

Church and State

The Lutheran State Church is the predominant Church in Norway, with 95 per cent of the population adhering to it. This status has historical causes. From the very introduction of Christianity to Norway, around year 1000, there has been a close connection — almost identity — between Church, people and state authorities. Christianity has, over the centuries, unified the people, created its moral and religious attitude, and still provides the basic values for legislation, ethical standards and view of man.

The present State Church system dates back to the introduction in 1537 of the Lutheran **Reformation,** by which the King and his officials took over the administration of the Church totally. The intention of this system — which Luther had accepted — was that the lay members should govern the Church, which in effect meant the King as «the most prominent lay member». In principle, therefore, this was a specific **Church government,** but over the years this distinction was not maintained and the system developed into a **State government of the Church.** Since the 1840's, a movement for reform of the Church administration to secure the «active Church people» greater participation in Church government has contributed to the formation of congregational councils (1920), diocesan councils (1933), The Church Council (1969), and the annual Conference of Bishops (1934) as organs within the Church administration. This line will probably be developed further. Serious proposals (1908 and, most recently, 1975) to dissolve the State Church system have, however, not received strong support within the Church itself nor within the people at large.

The system implies that all the «regular» work of the Church is administered and financed by the State or by municipalities. The King has the greatest responsibility in council with those among his cabinet members who — like himself — are members of the Church. The government organ for Church administration is the Ministry of Church and Education — indicating the close connection between Church and school in Norway. The school system started with church schools and religious instruction according to the Lutheran confession is still given to all pupils belonging to the State Church.

This system of Church administration does not interfere with the freedom of the ministers in respect of their work and preaching. Their spiritual authorities are the bishops of the Church. But the close connection between Church, State and people — which warrants the official name: **The Church of Norway** — has been critically questioned by some groups over the recent years.

The Lay Movement

Within the system of the State Church and its establishment and functioning as a broad «Church of the people», a more strict and pietistic lay movement has developed, with a marked call for personal conversion and more rigorous patterns of life. It goes back to several revivalist movements in the 19th century, the first and best known of these being led by the young peasant's son **Hans Nielsen Hauge** (1771—1824). In the second part of the century this movement organized itself into several «lay organizations» for «foreign» as well as «inner» missions, and with a more or less critical attitude to the «official» Church and its «mass religiosity». This does not prevent many of the leaders of the «lay organizations» from being ordained ministers, particularly in this century, or most of their members from taking part in the work of the official councils of the Church. It does not mean either that they wish to abolish the State-Church-system. The emphasis today is very much on the side of Christian education and milieu in addition to the more traditional revivalist preaching. The pietistic style of life is, however, maintained with some modifications, and the Bible is interpreted in a fairly fundamentalistic way — causing, for example, the rejection of female pastors by most of these organizations. Female ministry has been possible in the Church since 1938 and has been an established fact since 1961, although several of the bishops still refuse to ordain women and many congregations will not accept them.

Activities as "the Church of the People"

As a broad «Church of the people», the Church of Norway tries to reach all the people through its preaching and ministry, to revitalise the nominal Church members, and to create a Christian attitude in people and society. The Church of Norway had, in 1976, 10 bishops and 1112 ministers in «official» service. In 1975, these ministers conducted more than 67 000 worship services, 120 000 meetings, and 312 000 pastoral calls of different kinds. Almost all children are baptised and confirmed, 75 per cent of all weddings are performed by the Church (it must be remembered that most ministers refuse to marry couples where one or both parties have

been divorced), non-church funerals are extremely rare. There is specialised work going on, for example, for the Lapps, sailors, fishermen, students, the sick, the aged, prisoners, etc.

Church attendance at regular services is not satisfactory, and most of the nominal members do not take part in Church life nor engage themselves actively in the Christian faith and practice. To revitalise the nominal Church members into active participation, there are several opportunities given by the Church Council and other agencies, like the Institute for Christian Education, the Evangelical Academies, Church press, study and film institutions, to indicate the relevance of Christian faith and ethics to the problem of modern man.

The Free Churches

On the average, 5 000 persons leave the Church of Norway annually — most of them transferring to the numerous free Churches. Largest among them is the Pentecostal Movement (about 40 000 members), second in size is the Evangelical Lutheran Free Church. The Methodist Church, the Baptists, the Mission Covenant Church, the Roman Catholic Church and the Salvation Army are groups of some size, while the Anglican Church and the Eastern Orthodox Church are represented by small groups only. The immigration of foreign workers has changed the picture somewhat, and also introduced small groups of Muslims and other non-Christian religions.

Approximately 2 per cent of the population belong to no religious community. Some activities by these have been directed against the Church of Norway, in particular.

The Mass Media

THE DAILY PRESS

Norway has many newspapers in comparison with the population. The majority of them are small, both when compared with continental standards as well as with the other Nordic countries. But several copies are sold per inhabitant: only five or six countries are ahead of Norway in this respect in the world statistics. A good half of the newspapers are printed daily. They are also the largest newspapers. Those which constitute the top ten in terms of circulation also enjoy the widest geographical coverage. They often cover whole provinces, but they are not national dailies in the same sense as comparative large newspapers in other countries.

There are altogether 152 newspapers published in Norway. Of these, 72 are daily newspapers, which, in practice, means that they are published six times a week, since there are no Norwegian Sunday newspapers. The nucleus of well-established local newspapers with a modest circulation and limited catchment area, are at least equally characteristic of the Norwegian Press, and constitute a good half of the newspaper units. The news material of these newspapers is often limited, in the same way as the geographical coverage is, but they are warm spokesmen for their districts, and are often the secondary newspaper in households where two newspapers are taken. There are about 70 such newspapers in the country, which means that a comparatively large proportion of local districts are served by a newspaper which is written, produced and distributed in its own or adjacent district. During the course of the 1960's there was a stagnation in the total number of newspaper copies produced, and the introduction of regular television transmissions must take part of the blame. During recent years, however, there has been a discernible increase in newspaper sales.

The whole of the Norwegian Press is under private ownership. The principal organs for the Labour Party and the Communist Party are in a special position, since the parties themselves are the owners. The newspapers have differing ownership situations, from individual concerns which are dominated by large newspaper dynasties, to limited companies where the shareholders constitute more diffuse groups, and to companies where the shares are owned by the local Trade and Workers Union, as is the case with a large part of the Labour Press. There are just a few connections between the newspapers on the editorial side, while there is a definite and increasing level of cooperation between similarly disposed newspapers with regard to advertisements, distribution and marketing.

The State provides the newspapers with a measure of support, according to their size/market situation. There has been a certain voluntary cooperation between the newspapers over several years in respect of paper subsidies. From 1977 the State is also providing support to certain infrastructures: to research, further education and training of personnel and to individual cooperative measures which the Press has itself organized. A large part of the Press is bound politically, with declared loyalty to political parties, though normally without any formal bond. The Conservative Press is by far the largest and covers some of the biggest newspapers in the country. The Liberal

Press and Labour Press are approximately equally distributed, and these three together have control of more than 70% of the total circulation. The largest newspapers are: Aftenposten (ind. Conservative — Oslo) 215 000 copies., VG-Verdens Gang (ind. Conservative — Oslo) 152 000 copies., Dagbladet (Liberal — Oslo) 124 000 copies., Bergens Tidende (Liberal — Bergen) 81 000 copies.

RADIO AND TELEVISION

Radio and Television are both under the control of Norsk Rikskringkasting (Norwegian Broadcasting Corporation) according to the Law. This is an official institution which has been granted monopoly rights in this respect. NRK has a completely autonomous position in the Norwegian society: it is independent of both the Government and the administration, but is controlled by a council composed of representatives from the Storting, administration and other walks of life. The Head of Broadcasting is appointed by the Government. Radio and television are both under the control of the same main administration, but have separate administrations and programme productions. The guidelines for the management of the two media are principally the same, and they are subject to the same legal requirements. There are no detailed rules with regard to programme production for those who express themselves through these media. The Law contains general rules only, that broadcasting is to serve the whole country and that it has particular cultural and pedagogic duties. NRK transmits no commercial advertising or sponsored programmes. But it is normally expected that it will take good note of differing interests and give the best possible objective presentation of news and events. There are reasons to expect that a multi-channel radio system may be available in the 1980's. Broadcasting is now concentrating on an ambitious development of local district offices. These will enjoy a certain degree of autonomy, their own programme production, but will remain under the overall jurisdiction of the administration in Oslo. The district offices will serve the local population first and foremost.

Radio reached all Norwegian homes by the beginning of the fifties. It was almost thirty years before the whole country was covered. The changeover to FM radio took a far shorter time, and the whole country is now served by a very good transmission network. A couple of districts around the two largest towns are also engaged in stereo transmission trials. Television reaches practically all homes, — over 95% of them have television receivers, and the majority of those which are now sold are for coloured television.

Operation is financed via licences in respect of radio and television sets which are owned, and by means of a tax on the sales of these. Many programmes are subtitled. This is done out of consideration for those who are hard of hearing.

On the short wave there is a half hour programme every Sunday, with general information about Norway. Short Spanish newscasts are transmitted on Saturdays. There is otherwise a daily service by NRK in Norwegian for Norwegians abroad. This is a half hour programme which is transmitted eleven times a day, partly on the short wave and partly on the medium wave. The transmissions may be received on the 49m band and on the medium wave on 190 m and are broadcast every other hour from 1200 hours to 0800 hours local Norwegian time.

Outdoor Life

No one in Norway needs to travel far in order to reach the countryside. Just take a look at Oslo. Few capitals can offer their inhabitants facilities for out-of-door recreation like Oslo, which is surrounded by forests and peaceful lakes, covering about a quarter of a million acres. This area, which is called **Oslomarka,** has a network of innumerable ski trails during the winter and walking paths during the summer.

The sport of skiing is the national sport, and of the Nordic skiing disciplines cross-country skiing is the most popular. There are thousands of active ski-run competitors, and every Sunday during the winter there are ski-run meetings which attract skiers of virtually all categories and of all age groups up to 70 years and above. «Sport for all» is a slogan which has gained wide support in Norway. The lack of daylight is no obstacle where there are illuminated runs, and skiing in the evening has become popular.

Norwegians have become a «cabin-people» to an increasing degree. Many people own a cabin or second home in the country. On fine summer days the greatest exodus is in the direction of the sea. During the late summer, autumn, and winter, the mountains are more in demand. Freshwater fishing and mountaineering are sports for which the Norwegian countryside is particularly well suited. A quarter of the population are anglers — either as a hobby or a sport. It is still possible to find an angler's paradise in Norway. In rivers and lakes there are still salmon and trout to be found in great quantities, but it should be remebered by tourists that they have to obtain a fishing permit. The income which accrues from the sale of fishing permits is used for rational fish breeding. The hunter has many alternatives, — he may choose between many types of large and small game. It is estimated that about 1 300 000 animals are shot annually in Norway. Mountain peaks have challenged the skill and daring of climbers from all over the world. Some of the more spectacular first ascents have been made by French mountaineers. Both mountaineers as well as hikers, who prefer less exacting surroundings, will find a number of tourist cabins offering accommodation.

Competitive Sports

Sports play an increasingly important role in Norwegian society. No other sector of the country's cultural life is witness to such support and activity. The Norwegian Confederation of Sports (Norges Idrettsforbund), which is by far the largest voluntary organization in the country, has more than a million organized members. This means that every fourth Norwegian is a member of a sports club. Women's sports are flourishing as never before. There are 42 individual organizations which are affiliated with the parent association. By far the greatest of these is the Norwegian Football Association (which celebrated its 75th anniversary in 1977). Sports are given financial support by the Government, the means being provided by a State football pool company (Norsk Tipping) which has a monopoly on football betting in Norway. The high increase in the amount invested in football pools has benefitted sport to a great extent. The profits which accrue from football pools are earmarked for science and sport which both receive 50 per cent.

Cross-country skiing is a widely popular sport in Norway, and many thousands participate in competitions every year. Here is the skier Ivar Formo showing fine style.

Winter Sports

Skating (speed skating) has rich traditions in Norway, and Norwegian speed skaters have won 30 world championships, 34 European championships and 18 Olympic championships. The lack of ice-rinks must take some of the blame for the fact that figure skating lags behind in Norway.

With regard to the Nordic skiing disciplines (jumping and cross-country) Norway stands among the strongest nations in the world. The results of the Winter Olympics give an indication of the strength of Norwegian winter sports. During the years 1924—76, Norway won 50 Gold Medals and a total of 141 medals, more than any other single nation has won. Cross-country races and jumping contests are held regularly from December until April. Slalom and downhill are gaining increased support among young people.

The most important skiing event in Norway is the Holmenkollen Run, now known as the Holmenkollen Ski Festival, which attracts the best cross-country skiers and jumpers in the world — and 70 000 spectators to the skijumping. This is the most tradition-steeped ski run in the world, having been organized every year since 1892.

Sport of handicapped people can also be top-class sport, and there are many practitioners of these sports among Norwegian physically handicapped people who have acquitted themselves admirably in international events. Norway is a pioneering country with regard to sport for the handicapped. In the Ridderrennet (cross-country event), which was held in 1977 for the 14th time, 600 blind, partially blind and other physically handicapped people from 12 nations took part.

The skiing season in Norway extends from December to April.

Summer Sports

Football is incomparably the most popular summer sport in Norway, and is played throughout the whole country. First Division football (which includes 12 clubs) attracts 900 000 spectators during the April—October season. The Cup

Final is one of the major football events of the year. Norway does not belong to the leading football nations, but international matches always attract large crowds.

Handball is expanding rapidly, and this is a team sport which women have involved themselves in to a great extent. In the field of athletics Norway has produced several excellent specialist exponents.

Other summer sports include swimming, orienteering, cycling, sailing, rowing, canoing, kayak, tennis, badminton, golf, shooting, and archery.

Indoor sports such as boxing, wrestling, weightlifting and gymnastics, are popular. Volleyball and basketball are increasing in popularity. Judo and karate both have their adherents. Competitive ballroom dancing is also acknowledged as a sport. There is considerable interest in motor sports in Norway, and trotting and horseracing have a large and loyal following, not least of all because the races at the trotting and racecourses are tied up with on-course totalisator betting.

TOURISM

What tourists particularly value in Norway is the great sense of the natural surroundings, the cleanliness, the running waters and the immense variety. The majority of tourists travel around the country, therefore, in order to experience as much of this as possible. Because of this, the average stay at the hotels is 2 days per guest.

Even though the number of tourists may be considerable at the most popular tourist centres, it is not feasible to speak of mass-tourism.

New general guidelines in respect of Norwegian tourism policy have recently been evolved.

The main objective of tourism development is to create the correct circumstances which will afford Norwegians the best possible use of their holidays and free time. The extent of tourism promotion abroad will therefore be reduced, although overseas tourists will continue to be very welcome to share in the Norwegian tourism programme together with the country's own citizens. During the second half of this decade, slightly in excess of 60% of all overnight stays in recognised hotels were registered by Norwegians. The nomenclature 'hotel', 'tourist hotel', 'mountain hotel', 'motel' and 'restaurant' cannot be employed unless the buildings, equipment and management conforms with the requirements of the Hotel Management Act. Such establishments are also inspected by the Hotel and Tourism Directorate.

A good 79% of the hotels are open all the year, 7% have two seasons while 14% only operate during the summer.

The tourists spread themselves over wide areas of the country. The fjord country in the west, the coast of North Norway with the North Cape and the midnight sun as the most important attractions. Hiking holidays from cabin to cabin in the mountains and on the mountain plateaus has also become steadily more popular with foreigners. Hiring cabins by the coast, in the forest and up in the mountains has also become quite usual with foreigners, especially those from Northern Europe.

The majority of foreign tourists pass through Oslo, while Bergen and Trondheim are also visited a lot. A method of travel which is very much in demand is the coastal express (hurtigruten) which goes from Bergen and up to Kirkenes near the Russian frontier. On some trips it goes right up as far as Spitzbergen. A large number of cruise ships visit Norwegian fjords and towns, the North Cape and Spitzbergen.

Standard of Living

In 1975, Norway had the third largest Gross National Product per capita among the industrialised nations. Since the GNP in Norway is growing almost twice as fast as in Switzerland and Sweden, the two leading countries, Norway is expected to take the lead around 1980. The Norwegians themselves, however, treasure their easy access to unspoiled nature most of all. With only about 12 persons per square kilometre, Norway is the most sparsely populated country in Europe. Almost 20 per cent of the households own a second home, and about one third of the population enjoy using their own boats along the coast, sheltered by more than 100,000 islands. Pollution is low compared to most industrialised countries. The standard of health is among the highest in the world, and so is average life expectancy.

Traditionally, Norway has a very egalitarian society. Since the second World War, highly progressive taxes, together with social benefits, have added to the equalising of income. But most important is the rising demand for more skilled and better paid people. In the period 1946—73, transfers of income through taxes and social benefits doubled their share of real income. But during the same period, private disposable real income nearly trebled.

Peaceful labour relations are another characteristic. Together with Sweden, Norway lost fewer days due to strikes than any other OECD-nation in 1976. In a Norwegian survey published in 1976, a poll shows that more than 80 per cent of the wage earners almost never experience any disagreement with the management. Only about 2 per cent experience disagreement frequently.

In private consumption, a declining share of the food, beverages and tobacco sector shows that saturation point has been reached. At the same time, the share of travel, transportation — mainly private cars — and leisure is rising, from about 18 per cent in 1968 to an estimated 25 per cent i 1980.

Private cars have always been heavily taxed, and were uncommon until the beginning of the 1960's. From 1959 to 1976 the number of inhabitants per car fell from 21 to 4. By 1973, Norway was largely in line with the United Kingdom in passenger cars, telephones and television sets per 1 000 inhabitants — the numbers being 230, 329 and 249 respectively.

Inexpensive hydro-electricity, available to all but about 300 households, has boosted the number of home freezers, washing machines and other electrical appliances. Ninety two per cent of all households have refrigerators, and two-thirds have freezers. However, the number of private swimming pools is comparatively small.

The general standard of housing is high. By 1977, the number of dwellings built since the second world war reached almost one million, accommodation about 2/3 of the households. However, due to rising income and international migration, there is still a housing shortage, especially in the larger cities.

Fifty three per cent of dwellings are owner-occupied. The average number of rooms is 3.5 and 47 per cent of the houses are one-family dwellings. About 30 per cent of all households lack modern toilets, and 34 per cent are without separate bathrooms. But more than 98 per cent have running water.

Almost 80 per cent of the homes

are never bothered by noises or air pollution.

Norway has been a pioneer in industrial democracy. Self-governing production units were introduced in the early 1960's, and from the early 1970's all industrial enterprises with more than 50 employees have established employee representation in the leading organs.

None of the different representative systems secures the employees a majority, but even in early surveys 2/3 of the employee representatives expressed satisfaction with their influence.

Vital to this development are the egalitarian traditions laid down in the Constitution adopted in 1814, when Norway left Danish rule and abolished nobility. Puritanic heritage and enthusiasm for outdoor activities have also contributed to a joint concept of «the good life», among workers as well as managers and owners: hiking, cross-country skiing, boating, angling, vacationing in small cottages — and occasional charter tours to more sunny climes.

In North Norway in particular, the long, dark winters and bad weather constitute a strain.

In remote and sparsely populated areas, there are naturally incomplete cultural and social comforts. But road building and transport subsidies are steadily improving contact with regional centres where there are secondary schools, health services, and visits by travelling theatre groups and cinemas. Norway also has a wide variety of local and regional newspapers.

The interests of the individual are taken care of in many ways. The century-long practice of unrestricted right of way across water and uncultivated land has been secured by law. The Norwegian language has no word for trespassing.

Consumer protection was introduced in 1956 with the establishment of a special Ministry for Family and Consumer Affairs. Since then, a number of new agencies have been established, including the Consumer Council, the Committee for Declaration of Contents and Quality Marking, the State Institute of Consumer Research and Testing of Goods, as well as the Consumer Ombudsman and the Market Council.

The Consumer Council publishes a magazine, the Consumer Report, issued ten times annually with a circulation of 260,000. Including province offices, the Council handles close to 40,000 consumer complaints annually.

The Consumer Ombudsman registers 2,000 cases annually. In 20 per cent of the cases, the ombudsman acts on his own initiative. The other 80 per cent are based on private complaints. In 83 per cent of the cases, marketing is stopped or changed.

In 1972, consumer affairs were transferred to the new Ministry of Consumer Affairs and Government Administration. At the same time, a separate Ministry of Environment was established. Besides enforcing new anti-pollution standards, this ministry is responsible for permanent protection of particularly valuable natural and cultural environments, ranging from National Parks to Old Towns.

Four weeks vacation every year is established by law. But for housewives and livestock farmers, the official replacement services can cover only a fraction of the demand. For housewives, it is an emergency service, for cases of illness, twin births etc.

From 1959 to 1971, women increased their share of the representation in municipal assemblies from 6 to 15 per cent. But they find it hard to pursue political activities, as day institutions for children still cover only a minor part of the demand.

STANDARD OF LIVING

INDICATORS OF LIVING STANDARDS 1973—74

Per 1 000 inhabitants:				
	Norway	Sweden	UK	USA
Private cars	230	307	244	478
Telephones	329	594	340	657
TV sets	249	339	309	523
Doctors	1.5	1.5	1.3	1.7
Infant mortality	10.4	9.6	16.7	17.6
(per 1 000 live births).				

Women are also subjected to economic discrimination, in spite of official declarations about equal pay for equal work. By using different names for virtually the same jobs, and through hiring practices, the average pay in industry is about 20 per cent lower for women, compared with the average for men. In addition, women serve in the majority of low-paid jobs in commerce and other services.

In a 1973 White Paper discussing the use of oil revenues, it was declared that the price target is to create a society with a higher «life quality». Economic incentives will be used to replace old, polluting and physically and mentally stressing activities with «intelligence industry». More capital can be invested to create better paid and more meaningful and rewarding jobs.

The main aims also include a wider choice of jobs for women, and for handicapped people. Norway is already a leading nation in the efforts to retain and employ the handicapped. Following training in special, smaller factories, the handicapped are to be integrated in the regular workforce as far as possible.

Traffic accidents increased with the number of private cars, but in the late 1970's the trend has been reversed. In 1975 the figures were 537 traffic deaths and 3 437 injured.

The crime rate has risen sharply in Norway in recent years, but is still low by international standards, particularly concerning violent crimes. Crimes investigated by police rose from 10 per 1 000 inhabitants in 1958 to 14 in 1968 and 22 in 1973.

The negative side of the «welfare state» includes the increased limitation of some individual liberties, and a feeling of being «nannied». The extensive transfers of income necessitate income tax rates of more than 50 per cent on overtime pay, even for people with a normal income.

But the «welfare state» is supported by a wide majority. Only one very small political party works for reversing the trend. By international standards, the poll at the national elections is high, usually around 80 per cent.

Books on Norway in English

Askeland, Jan: Norwegian painting. A survey. Oslo 1971, Tanum.

Helvig, Magne og Viggo Johannesen: Norway. Land—people—industries. A brief geography. Oslo 1974, Tanum.

Jerman, Gunnar: New Norway. 1976. Published by the Export council of Norway. Oslo 1976, Grøndahl.

Lange, Kristian: Norwegian music. A survey. Oslo 1971, Tanum.

Midgaard, John: A brief history of Norway. Oslo 1976, Tanum.

Nesheim, Asbjørn: Introducing the Lapps. Oslo 1977, Tanum.

Parmann, Øistein: Norwegian sculpture. Oslo 1969, Dreyer.

Welle-Strand, Erling: Tourist in Norway. Oslo 1974, Schibsted.

721 25 178 2500